Exercise Booklet

Cy Strom

Harold Nelson

Quick Access
Reference for Writers

Fourth Canadian Edition

Lynn Quitman Troyka
Douglas Hesse
with the assistance of
Cy Strom

Pearson Canada
Toronto

Original edition published by Pearson Education, Inc., Upper Saddle River, New Jersey, USA. Copyright © 2010 by Pearson Education, Inc. This edition is authorized for sale only in Canada.

ISBN 978-0-205-03058-3

Acquisitions Editor: David S. Le Gallais
Sponsoring Editor: Carolin Sweig
Developmental Editor: Megan Burns
Lead Project Manager: Söğüt Y. Güleç
Production Editor: Avivah Wargon

1 2 3 4 5   15 14 13 12 11

Printed and bound in Canada.

PREFACE FOR STUDENTS

Lynn Troyka writes about the power and freedom that knowledge gives each of us: "Students are empowered by knowledge, for it frees us all to enjoy the pleasures of language and to fulfill, with energy and joy, our potentials as writers."

We have kept this idea in mind while writing this Exercise Booklet. We want the booklet to help you master the information in *Quick Access* in Grammar Basics, Sentences and Words, Punctuation and Mechanics, and Tips for Multilingual Writers. By increasing your knowledge in this way, you will grow in the freedom, power, and joy you feel when you write.

This booklet contains sets of exercises for specific sections in *Quick Access*. Each set contains five lettered exercises—with answers at the back of this booklet—and ten numbered exercises.

You will learn best if you review the appropriate section(s) immediately before you do a set of exercises. Keep in mind the ideas you have just read as you complete the exercises.

Practice does not necessarily make perfect, but it does make better. The practice you do in this book should help you grow as a writer.

PREFACE FOR INSTRUCTORS

Many of us who use Lynn Quitman Troyka's *Quick Access Reference for Writers*, Fourth Canadian Edition, in our classes probably need exercises for quizzes, tests, homework, individualized instruction, supplementary material in a writing lab, questions for contests during class sessions, projections or displays on which we demonstrate how to solve specific problems, or training material for peer tutors. Having the exercises already written saves us preparation time.

This booklet meets the need. It contains sets of supplementary exercises for four sections of *Quick Access*, in the order in which they appear in its current fourth edition: Grammar Basics, Sentences and Words, Punctuation and Mechanics, and Tips for Multilingual Writers. Five review exercise sets addressing problems at the level of words and sentences follow the Tips for Multilingual Writers section.

Each set contains fifteen exercises. The first five exercises in each set are lettered, and the next ten are numbered. Answers for the lettered exercises start on page 76 in this booklet. Answers for numbered exercises are in a separate Answer Key available for downloading from the Pearson Canada website at **vig.pearsoned.ca**; contact your local sales representative for details and access.

CONTENTS

TIPS FOR MULTILINGUAL WRITERS

vi

GRAMMAR BASICS: 41b—Identifying Pronouns

Underline all pronouns in the following sentences.

EXAMPLE:

I said it myself.

a.   Give it to me.

b.   Give the ball to me.

c.   Would anybody like to help me eat the pizza?

d.   This is Jordan's running shoe.

e.   Please return the shoe to Jordan.

1.   Mercury is a silvery-white metallic element; it is poisonous.

2.   Although it is a metal, mercury is liquid at room temperatures.

3.   Mercury's melting point is about 39°C; it turns to liquid at that temperature.

4.   Mercury is also called quicksilver.

5.   While they were working with it in the laboratory, Heather and Samita handled the mercury very carefully.

6.   Because the planet Mercury is so close to the sun, it is very hot.

7.   It is named after Mercury, who was the fleet-footed messenger of the Roman gods.

8.   Mercury, which goes around the sun in eighty-eight days, has the shortest orbit of all the planets in the solar system.

9.   We can occasionally see Mercury as a morning or an evening star.

10.   This is a planet scheduled for a visit by a Japanese-European space probe in 2020.

GRAMMAR BASICS: 41j—Subjects and Predicates

Underline subjects once and verbs twice in the following sentences.

EXAMPLE:

Roberto ordered a soft drink.

a.   The visitors said goodbye.

b.   They stood for a long time in the doorway.

c.   They seemed sad about leaving.

d.   The longer they stayed, the sadder I became.

e.   I was tired, and I wanted them to leave.

1.   Two residents of the dormitory were up on the roof.

2.   They had climbed a tree, and they had hoisted themselves onto a gargoyle.

3.   Weeks of planning had led to their escapade.

4.   Janis and Ravi saw them in the moonlight.

5.   Ravi e-mailed his brother about it the next day.

6.   The dog chased the cat.

7.   My neighbour owns both animals.

8.   He normally keeps them apart.

9.   Unfortunately, he forgot to shut the door to the house.

10. The dog and the cat ran into the house and knocked over two lamps.

GRAMMAR BASICS: 42a—Transitive and Intransitive Verbs

Underline transitive verbs once and intransitive verbs twice in the following sentences.

EXAMPLE:

Jane talked to Mark as she scribbled me a note.

a.   Jane talked slowly today.

b.   She spoke too rapidly when she gave her speech yesterday.

c.   The professor leaned forward and listened yesterday.

d.   I am happy that she spoke slowly.

e.   When I give speeches, I speak slowly.

1.   Christopher Marlowe wrote the sixteenth-century English play *Doctor Faustus*.

2.   In Goethe's *Faust*, Mephistopheles tempts Faust.

3.   Faust sells his soul to the powers of darkness.

4.   Charles Gounod's opera *Faust* is about the same story.

5.   Gounod wrote his opera in 1859.

6.   Judge Emily Murphy worked for women's rights.

7.   She was a campaigner for full political rights for women.

8.   In 1929, she won the right for women's membership in the Senate.

9.   The "Persons Case" is the name of Murphy's challenge to the Constitution.

10.   She died in Edmonton in 1933.

GRAMMAR BASICS: 42b—Regular and Irregular Verbs

Revise verbs in the following sentences if necessary.

EXAMPLE:

        supposed
My shoes were ~~suppose~~ to be polished.

a.   I dived off the high board.

b.   Have you ever dove off the high board?

c.   I was a little shook up by the experience.

d.   Until recently, I would have sank in water over my head.

e.   I have grew stronger as a swimmer in recent weeks.

1.   Concita has wore a toque to school ever since Halloween.

2.   She swored to dress warmly this winter.

3.   I asked what lead her to chose a toque and not a fur hat with earmuffs.

4.   In reply, she asked where she could have finded a fur hat with the logo of the Edmonton Oilers on it.

5.   Ron has been readying his rich uncle for his latest request.

6.   He sworn to get the latest Apple product before Jade got one.

7.   Ron's uncle should have knew that it's not just a toy.

8.   Ron seen a demonstration of the device's remarkable processing power.

9.   He has even wrote a paper on the productivity possibilities of media-rich platforms.

10.   Writing the paper earned Ron an A and begun his campaign to impress his rich uncle.

4

GRAMMAR BASICS: 42b–c—Main and Auxiliary Verbs

Underline main verbs once and auxiliary verbs twice in the following sentences.

EXAMPLE:

Jane <u><u>might</u> <u>talk</u></u> to Mark.

a. It is claimed that the first snowboard was a cafeteria food tray that a mischievous student swiped.

b. By 1980, professional snowboards were being manufactured.

c. The Olympics admitted snowboarding as an official event in 1998.

d. The first gold medal was awarded to Ross Rebagliati, who failed a drug test just minutes afterward.

e. Rebagliati would have lost his medal if Canadian officials had not noticed the absence of any Olympic ban against that particular drug.

1. In a democracy, power is vested in the people.

2. People in a very tiny democracy might rule directly.

3. More commonly, people in a democracy will elect representatives.

4. These representatives can rule for the people.

5. Some countries, including Canada, have combined democracy with monarchy.

6. Does monarchy contradict the principle of democracy?.

7. Our queen or king is never elected.

8. There is little support here for the abolition of the monarchy, however.

9. This contrasts with the situation in Australia.

10. Since the 1950s, our elected prime minister has chosen a Canadian citizen as the monarch's representative.

GRAMMAR BASICS: 42b, 42d—Irregular Verbs Including lie and lay

Revise verbs in the following sentences if necessary.

EXAMPLE:

fell
I ~~fall~~ down the stairs yesterday.

a. Has Tera Van Beilen swam in her event yet?

b. For weeks, Oakville's Van Beilen has looked like a sure bet for the gold medal.

c. After a hard practice, the junior team laid down in an exhausted heap.

d. Canada has became a force in swimming in the Youth Olympics.

e. Rachel Nicol from Lethbridge faught off the competition to win bronze in the same event.

1. I awoken feeling refreshed.

2. Sarah brought her notebook to the chemistry professor.

3. Had you began to do the experiment?

4. Sarah had already took two years of chemistry before switching majors.

5. We run out of sugar, so we could bake only three dozen donuts.

6. The left winger blowed by the defence and put a shot right on net.

7. Maria shook up a can of tomato juice and added it to the mix.

8. Have you lay the books on your desk?

9. I am laying down to rest.

10. Given the weather report, we should have wore our snowshoes.

GRAMMAR BASICS: 42e—Verb Tenses

Use the tense indicated in parentheses when revising the verbs in the following sentences.

EXAMPLE:

I see the sign.   (past)   I saw the sign.

a.   I walk.   (future perfect)

b.   I walk.   (past)

c.   I walk.   (past perfect progressive)

d.   I walk.   (present progressive)

e.   I walk.   (future progressive)

1.   They sing.   (future perfect)

2.   They sing.   (future progressive)

3.   They sing.   (future perfect progressive)

4.   They sing.   (future)

5.   They sing.   (past)

6.   We sit.   (present perfect)

7.   We sit.   (present progressive)

8.   We sit.   (present perfect progressive)

9.   We sit.   (past perfect progressive)

10.   We sit.   (past)

GRAMMAR BASICS: 42e–g—Verb Tense, Mood, and Voice

Revise the verbs in the following sentences if necessary.

EXAMPLES:

covered

The temperature has dropped sharply since the clouds ~~cover~~ the sun.

dropped

The temperature ~~was dropped~~ when the clouds covered the sun.

a. Joan of Arc was a French military leader in the fifteenth century who says that God spoke to her in voices.

b. Shortly after the army she led forced the English troops to end their siege of Orleans in 1429, she watched the coronation of Charles VII.

c. If Joan of Arc would have lived in the twenty-first century, her videos probably would have gone viral.

d. I wish that time travel was possible, so I could meet her.

e. The meeting of Joan of Arc by me I would find interesting.

1. The planet Neptune was discover in 1846.

2. Before Neptune's discovery, astronomers observe that the planet Uranus sometimes sped up and sometimes slowed down as it orbited the sun.

3. The astronomers theorizes that the gravitational pull of another planet caused this uneven movement.

4. This theory was confirmed by the sighting of Neptune by astronomers.

5. The planet Neptune is named after the Roman god of the sea, Neptune; astronomers use his fishing spear, the trident, as the planet's symbol.

6. Dr. Chang would have moved to a small town if she would have found a good teaching hospital there.

7. She will have helped many people recover by the time she retired.

8. If Dr. Chang was not going to retire next year, I would ask her to be my family physician.

9. I suggest that Leon finds himself a family doctor soon.

10. Unless he were to stop visiting the emergency ward for minor medical problems, he will drain resources from the health care system.

GRAMMAR BASICS: 43—Singular and Plural Subjects

Underline singular subjects once and plural subjects twice in the following sentences.

EXAMPLE:

Tecumseh was a Shawnee.

a. Gargoyles were used on many buildings during the Middle Ages.

b. A gargoyle is a sculpture depicting a grotesque or fantastic creature.

c. Measles can be deadly.

d. The jury voted "guilty" and "not guilty" in equal numbers on the first vote.

e. Anyone who has something to say should speak up now.

1. Economics was dominated by the doctrine of mercantilism for several hundred years after the decline of feudalism.

2. A nation's wealth, in this doctrine, was based mainly on the amount of gold and silver in the nation's treasury.

3. Accumulating gold and silver bullion, establishing colonies, developing a strong merchant marine, and encouraging mining and industry were all approaches nations used to develop favourable balances of trade.

4. All mercantilist countries of the Western world shared a common goal: to achieve a surplus of exports over imports in order to build the national wealth.

5. This doctrine encouraged European countries to develop colonial holdings in Asia, Africa, North America, and South America.

6. Hydrogen, the lightest of all the chemical elements, normally has as its atom one electron in orbit around one proton.

7. A star, as well as a hydrogen bomb, produces a fusion reaction that transforms hydrogen atoms into helium atoms.

8. This fusion releases huge amounts of energy.

9. On earth, hydrogen is usually found as a gas.

10. No other element in the universe is as abundant as hydrogen.

GRAMMAR BASICS: 43—Subject–Verb Agreement

Revise the following sentences, if necessary, to make subjects and verbs agree.

EXAMPLE:

are
They ~~is~~ talking.

a. George Lucas's *Star Wars* have had several sequels.

b. Some of the buses is overheated.

c. Across the street is a bus stop.

d. The worst part of riding a bus are the waiting.

e. Two dollars are the current bus fare.

1. Chief among his good qualities are his sense of humour.

2. The baseball team is scattered across the field, shagging flies and doing wind sprints.

3. One of the issues we covered are racial discrimination.

4. Liver and onions are not one of my favourite foods.

5. Seventy-five dollars were all I had in my savings account.

6. Françoise, as well as her two karate instructors, are very disciplined.

7. Neither Françoise nor her instructors has ever had to visit the campus first aid centre.

8. Each of the instructors have a black belt.

9. At least 640 megabytes of RAM are needed to perform those functions.

10. The film society has 117 students in it.

GRAMMAR BASICS: 44a–i—Pronoun–Antecedent Agreement and Pronoun Reference

Revise the following sentences, if necessary, so that each pronoun clearly refers to and agrees with the correct antecedent.

EXAMPLE:

The   books.
~~Each of the~~ students opened their ~~book.~~

a.   I expect to find something interesting in any song credited to Lennon and McCartney, but I'm no fan of what he wrote after John Lennon's death.

b.   I like to study biological trivia; that is my major.

c.   In Saskatchewan, they say that the cold is a dry cold.

d.   Either the server or my mobile phone has lost its signal.

e.   The band put away its instruments.

1.   I waited at the bus stop until it came.

2.   When you take into account the health implications, frequent hand washing makes sense.

3.   Was it the Canadian short story writer Mavis Gallant that wrote a book about the French student revolt of May 1968?

4.   The skateboard that I want to buy is on sale.

5.   Every dog and cat in the vet's waiting room cowered nervously at their owner's feet.

6.   Once upon a time, a happy couple went to Niagara Falls for their honeymoon; but we know that the last time such a thing happened was in 1964.

7.   Each of the applicants filled out their own form and paid their fee.

8.   Anyone who wants to can open their presents on Christmas Eve.

9.   The audience settled into its seats as the curtain rose.

10. Every member of the audience were happy.

GRAMMAR BASICS: 44j–s—Pronoun Case

Revise pronouns in the following sentences if necessary.

EXAMPLE:

He
~~Him~~ and I are on the soccer team.

a. John, Zara, and me ate the pizza.

b. The anchovies were ordered by Zara and I.

c. Us anchovy lovers spare no effort to get our favourite condiment included in the order.

d. Who needs John's opinion, anyway?

e. The next pizza may be a joint effort by only Zara and myself, however.

1. She and him tried the new vegetarian burrito place.

2. Burgers no longer appeal to her and I.

3. She and myself were happy to discover a new falafel vendor on campus.

4. Our professor expects him and I to win the scholarships.

5. I'm sure that one of the winners will be me.

6. The instructors theirselves are celebrating their students' success.

7. Whomever gave you that information was wrong.

8. Rising book prices are a problem all of us students face.

9. To who should I speak about admission to law school?

10. Lawrence showed his paintings to my sister and myself.

GRAMMAR BASICS: 45—Adjectives

Underline all adjectives in the following sentences.

EXAMPLE:

She felt <u>happy</u>.

a. The old computer is unreliable.

b. My father is thrifty and conservative.

c. The desktop—old, outdated, and decrepit—belongs to my father.

d. It was a fast computer when he first bought it.

e. It holds many files he still needs for work.

1. Members of the winning team are usually happier than members of the losing team.

2. Unblanched celery is greener than blanched celery.

3. We bought the most expensive meal at the restaurant.

4. Lana's laptop is fast.

5. Lana's laptop is faster than Ulla's laptop.

6. Lana's laptop is the fastest laptop in the entire class.

7. Lana's expensive laptop runs beautifully.

8. You look well.

9. You write well.

10. He looked in alarm at the phone's fading screen.

GRAMMAR BASICS: 45—Adverbs

Underline all adverbs in the following sentences.

EXAMPLE:

The cook felt <u>unusually</u> creative <u>today</u>.

a. The fireplace was very hot.

b. The high temperature for that day was twenty below zero.

c. We regularly pushed huge maple logs into the fireplace.

d. The wind rattled the windowpanes, and the snow swirled fiercely outside the house.

e. The bare trees swayed ominously in the twilight.

1. Mary's performance in the basketball game was truly memorable.

2. She ran more rapidly than the other centre.

3. She also jumped higher than the other centre.

4. Mary played memorably.

5. Mary played well.

6. The family room is the most frequently used room in our house.

7. Clearly, the basement is underutilized.

8. Today, the family room was insufferably hot.

9. The thermostat apparently was broken.

10. The service technician is currently working on the thermostat.

GRAMMAR BASICS: 45b–e—Using Adjectives and Adverbs

Revise adjectives and adverbs in the following sentences if necessary.

EXAMPLE:

                    fewer
This cheesecake contains ~~less~~ calories than regular cheesecake.

a.   The tortoise crawled slowly.

b.   There wasn't no way to hurry the tortoise.

c.   This tortoise is real slow.

d.   The tortoise in the Metro Zoo is the most ugliest tortoise I've ever seen.

e.   That ugly tortoise also smells badly.

1.   Beth is the most happy runner on the team.

2.   Beth ran rapid.

3.   She ran good.

4.   Beth took less drinks of water during the race than the other athletes.

5.   She ran the best race she has ever run.

6.   She won the race because the other runners didn't have no finishing kick.

7.   The trophy she won looks well in her room.

8.   Even when she was in grade school, Beth was the most swift person in her class.

9.   She was more swifter than her brother

10.   She was the most swiftest runner in grade six.

SENTENCES: 46—Sentence Fragments

Revise the following, if necessary, to eliminate any fragments.

EXAMPLE:

Cartoonists are publishing a wider range of books than ever before, in various media, sometimes treating serious subjects. Such as Chester Brown's award-winning book about Métis leader Louis Riel.

Cartoonists are publishing a wider range of books than ever before, in various media. Some treat serious subjects, such as Chester Brown's award-winning book about Métis leader Louis Riel.

a. What is the difference between a cat and a sentence? A cat has claws at the end of its paws, and a sentence has a pause at the end of its clause.

b. Today, *girl* denotes a female child. In Middle English, *girl* a child of either sex.

c. The word *balkanization* derives from the name of the Balkan Peninsula, which was divided into several small nations. In the early twentieth century.

d. Bacteria, at times present in incorrectly canned or preserved foods, causes botulism, a type of food poisoning. Which is often fatal if not treated properly.

e. The title character in *Prince of Persia*. Played by Jake Gyllenhaal.

1. A big dark ring of sesame-covered Turkish bread. Called *simit*.

2. Turkish salads contain vegetables that Canadians associate with Italy. They also often contain ingredients that Canadians associate with countries east of Turkey.

3. A dozen words for *peat*. In the Irish language.

4. The Irish language was revived. After Ireland became an independent republic.

5. Politicians in Ireland. In certain circumstances, expected to speak at least a few words of Irish.

6. In the late 1970s. Scott Olson designed improvements for in-line skates.

7. In-line skates and skateboards. Since then have become extremely popular.

8. Joni Mitchell, a self-taught musician. On many lists of the most creative guitar stylists.

9. In the early seventeenth century. Henry Hudson explored Hudson Bay.

10. In computer science, a bit is the smallest unit of information. A blend of b(inary) and (dig)it.

SENTENCES: 47—Comma Splices and Fused Sentences

Revise the following sentences to eliminate comma splices and fused sentences.

EXAMPLE:

                          and
I bought the tickets,   we attended the concert.
                    ∧

a. William Lyon Mackenzie King successfully held office longer than any other Canadian prime minister he left an ambiguous legacy.

b. The huge majority that John Diefenbaker won for the Progressive Conservatives in 1958 has not left him with a victorious reputation only five years later his government collapsed.

c. Kim Campbell and John Turner stayed in office for only a few months after inheriting power from comparatively successful predecessors.

d. Pierre Trudeau preceded Turner as prime minister, Brian Mulroney was the leader who retired in favour of Campbell.

e. During Diefenbaker's last year in office, writer Peter C. Newman criticized him severely in a book called *Renegade in Power,* the same writer released a book in 2005 that deeply offended Mulroney.

1. Some people frown on gambling, many phrases in English originally were associated with gambling.

2. We refer to taking responsibility when we say "The buck stops here," the phrase was originally used in poker games in the 1800s.

3. The dealer in the poker game passed a knife with a handle made of buck horn to another player, that person became the new dealer.

4. *Passing the buck* had a literal origin it meant passing the knife (and the deal).

5. White, red, and blue chips are used for betting in poker, with blue chips being the most valuable, similarly, blue-chip stocks on the stock market are normally the most stable, secure, and valuable.

6. Bridge can be played for money it is such a complex game that some people play it mostly to show off their skill.

18

7.   Bridge players count their winnings in points, poker players, however, usually count theirs in chips or in cash.

8.   Many students are introduced to bridge in university, not all continue to play it after they graduate.

9.   Like poker, bridge is a game that leaves an important place for deceit, bluffing in bridge is different from bluffing in poker.

10. A poker player's unreadable poker face misleads opponents in betting, this tactic differs from a bridge player's strategy of fooling opponents into playing the wrong cards.

SENTENCES: 48—Problems with Sentence Shifts

Revise the following sentences if necessary.

EXAMPLE:

      people visit
When ~~a person visits~~ Banff National Park, they should do a lot of walking.

a.   When I hear people argue over PCs versus Macs, you'd think they were arguing over their religious beliefs.

b.   According to Mae West, "Too much of a good thing can be wonderful."

c.   By standing inside the penalty area allows a soccer goalie to handle the ball.

d.   The Montreal Royals sent the first black player to be joining a major-league baseball team.

e.   One reason that the year 2010 was important is because several new networks began competing with Canada's big three wireless corporations then.

1.   A private citizen may legally make an arrest if they have observed a crime or have reasonable cause to believe a crime has been committed.

2.   The more a person studies a foreign language, the better they should expect to speak it.

3.   Many students expect to find jobs in their major fields eventually, but some problems are probably anticipated.

4.   The majority of the students in my political science class identified three main goals for government: preserve the health-care system, protect the environment, and an end to corruption.

5.   By working out makes an individual physically fit.

6.   The first thing I did today was when I logged on to check the hockey scores.

7.   The purpose of the Confederation Bridge was built to join Prince Edward Island to the mainland.

8.   As your medical doctor, I am not impressed with your health strategy of watching every hockey game on every cable channel.

9.   Canada is where there is the most coastline in a country.

10.   I think that Wikipedia will one day be the world's greatest encyclopedia, but when that day will come is not known to me.

SENTENCES: 49—Misplaced Modifiers

Revise misplaced modifiers in the following sentences if necessary.

EXAMPLE:

         completely
How the police officer   subdued the violent suspect ~~completely~~ amazed me.
           ^

a.   The shepherd's dog ran loudly barking toward the sheep.

b.   The shepherd signalled her dog to herd the sheep, anxious to go home.

c.   The shepherd wanted her dog to quickly herd the sheep home and to leave no stragglers.

d.   The shepherd just had bought her dog from a neighbouring rancher.

e.   Until home, the dog herded the sheep diligently.

1.   Held in a giant lecture hall, my roommate attended his first psychology lecture last week.

2.   Lewis was eager to learn more about the research done by the lecturer that was the topic of his high-school essay last spring.

3.   He immediately recognized this professor's name from last year's school text.

4.   Two dozen students shoved their way ahead of Lewis, who was standing at the door, determined to get the best seats.

5.   How could Lewis have known that he needed so aggressively to claim his seat?

6.   In choosing my first-year courses, my course adviser suggested that I should look at class size as one criterion.

7.   Always ready to take good advice, that explains how I came to walk into a nearly empty seminar room on the first day of classes.

8.   A young lecturer who only had earned her doctorate the year before was with enthusiasm talking about her specialty.

9.   Leaning over the lectern and gesturing with both hands, the subject she was discussing was seventeenth-century Dutch literature.

10.   Lewis intends still to complete a degree in psychology, but my course of study is for the next four years less certain.

21

SENTENCES: 50—Conciseness

Revise the following sentences for conciseness if necessary.

EXAMPLE:

The jacket is red. ~~in colour~~.
 ^

a.   As a matter of fact, I liked the movie.

b.   Our landlord made a decision to paint our windowsills.

c.   There are eight of us who share the house.

d.   John, who is a good athlete, wants to play professional football.

e.   The bill that was introduced in Parliament was introduced by a backbencher.

1.   Let there be no doubt about it, this government is no longer corrupt, today or in the future.

2.   As a matter of fact, statistics show that in the case of the generation of baby-boomers, most baby-boomers invest conservatively.

3.   A conservative investment is the type of investment that will not decrease in value.

4.   Whichever playwright it is who wrote that play is an extremely keen student of people's human emotions.

5.   Your completion of the paper several days before it is due will result in an opportunity for your relaxation immediately before handing in the paper.

6.   There are five different meal plans offered by the food service.

7.   *The Pale Horse*, which is a detective novel, was written by Agatha Christie.

8.   Louis Riel, who was a Métis, led the Métis, his people, in two different rebellions in the Prairies of western Canada.

9.   The conflict between the Métis people and those people who were opposed to them encompassed language, religion, and way of life.

10. The tutorial leader's suggestion to Imelda is that she should pay a visit to the library if she wants to learn how to use online sources with proper effectiveness.

22

SENTENCES: 50—Conciseness

Revise the following sentences for conciseness if necessary.

EXAMPLE:

old.
The car was dirty, rusty, and ~~it had been manufactured many years ago.~~

a.   The house was large, old, and it had drafts.

b.   Michael Moore, a filmmaker who is an American, sometimes presents Canada as a kind of utopian society in the movies that he makes.

c.   The bottom line is the line that shows profit or loss.

d.   People often extend this literal meaning of bottom line, and they use the phrase to mean the determining consideration in a decision.

e.   Although Canadians laugh at Michael Moore's portrayal of Canada, the bottom line is that they feel flattered by the portrayal.

1.   My library carrel is small and cramped, but it has the quality of being well lit.

2.   I am on a waiting list of two months for a book that is important and that a faculty professor has signed out.

3.   I finally found the text on Canadian history that was assigned.

4.   I read the first chapter in it, and I think I've decided on the paper that I'm going to be writing.

5.   Rather than writing on the Canadian Pacific Railway, instead I'll concentrate on issues surrounding the career of Louis Riel.

6.   Louis Riel, who defied the government of John A. Macdonald, was hanged in 1885.

7.   Riel was a Métis leader from the Prairies, and most of the people he led were also Métis from the Prairies.

8.   Riel displayed charisma and vision, and the Métis of Manitoba and Saskatchewan valued the qualities of charisma and vision in a leader.

23

9. Elected as an MP to Parliament in 1873 and 1874, Riel also led his people in battle against the opponents who stood against them.

10. It seems that Riel's execution remains controversial.

SENTENCES: 51a–b—Coordination

Combine the following sentences to illustrate coordination. Do not show coordination in the same way in two successive sentences. Add or delete words or punctuation marks, but do no major rewriting.

EXAMPLE:

The sky became dark. The moon rose.

The sky became dark, and the moon rose.

a. The French Revolution began in 1789. It ended France's thousand-year monarchy.

b. Louis XVI assembled the Estates General to deal with France's huge debt. The common people's part of the Estates General proclaimed itself France's true legislature.

c. Louis protested. A crowd destroyed the Bastille.

d. A constitutional monarchy was established. Some people thought the king would be content.

e. Louis and the queen, Marie Antoinette, tried to leave the country. They were caught, convicted of treason, and executed.

1. On the Pacific coast, butter clams are popular. On the Atlantic coast, soft-shell clams and quahogs are favoured.

2. Littleneck clams are small. They are the tenderest Atlantic hardshells.

3. Surf clams are Pacific hardshells. They are larger and tougher than littlenecks.

4. Littlenecks are normally steamed. Surf clams are normally minced for chowder or cut into strips for frying.

5. The Atlantic provides most of the commercial clams caught in Canada. The Pacific provides fewer and less common varieties.

6. Transatlantic flights used to refuel at Gander, Newfoundland. Many immigrants caught their first sight of Canada at Gander.

7. Other immigrants first set foot on Halifax's Pier 21. Halifax was not the only immigrant seaport.

8. Quebec City accepted immigrants by sea. In the nineteenth century, many landed on nearby Grosse Île.

9. Your ancestors may have come to one of these ports. They may have arrived at another..

10. Your family may have flown into Toronto's Pearson International Airport. Many new Canadians land there.

SENTENCES: 51c–d—Subordination

Combine the following sentences to illustrate subordination. Do not show subordination in the same way in two successive sentences. Add or delete words or punctuation marks, but do no major rewriting. For items a–e, the event in the first sentence occurred before the event in the second.

EXAMPLE:

The sky became dark. The moon rose.

After the sky became dark, the moon rose.

a.   The French Revolution began in 1789. It ended France's thousand-year monarchy.

b.   King Louis XVI assembled the Estates General to deal with France's huge debt. The common people's part of the Estates General proclaimed itself France's true legislature.

c.   King Louis protested. A crowd destroyed the Bastille.

d.   A constitutional monarchy was established. Some people thought the king would be content.

e.   King Louis and the queen, Marie Antoinette, tried to leave the country. They were caught, convicted of treason, and executed.

1.   On the Pacific coast, butter clams are popular. On the Atlantic coast, soft-shell clams and quahogs are favoured.

2.   Littleneck clams are small. They are the tenderest Atlantic hardshells.

3.   Surf clams are Pacific hardshells. They are larger and tougher than littlenecks.

4.   Littlenecks are normally steamed. Surf clams are normally minced for chowder or cut into strips for frying.

5.   The Atlantic provides most of the commercial clams caught in Canada. The Pacific provides fewer and less common varieties.

6.   Transatlantic flights used to refuel at Gander, Newfoundland. Many immigrants caught their first sight of Canada at Gander.

7.   Other immigrants first set foot on Halifax's Pier 21. Halifax was not the only immigrant seaport

8. Quebec City accepted immigrants by sea. In the nineteenth century, many landed on nearby Grosse Île.

9. Your ancestors may have come to one of these ports. Your family may have arrived after the age of the great passenger boats.

10. Your family may have flown into Toronto's Pearson International Airport. Many new Canadians land there.

SENTENCE STYLE: 52a–d—Parallelism

Revise any sentences showing faulty parallelism.

EXAMPLE:

attending

Professor Singh recommends studying the text and ~~to attend~~ class.

a. Archimedes was an ancient Greek scientist, mathematician, and he made inventions.

b. According to legend, Archimedes is supposed to have said both "Give me the place to stand and a lever long enough, and I will move the earth" and to have shouted "Eureka!" when he stepped into his bath and realized that he could measure the volume of an object by determining the volume of the water it displaces when submerged.

c. Archimedes discovered the principle of buoyancy, he discovered formulas for calculating the areas of various geometric figures, and he is remembered as the inventor of the Archimedean screw.

d. According to the principle of buoyancy, a boat floats and balloons will rise because they weigh less than the water or air they displace.

e. Math students still study the formulas Archimedes discovered in geometry, and engineering students still study his ideas about applying geometry to hydrostatics and mechanics.

1. I've felt tired, grumpy, and with an upset stomach.

2. My doctor recommends that I lose five kilograms, exercise each day, and to sleep at least seven hours each night.

3. I'll follow my doctor's advice because I want to look better and because I want to be feeling better.

4. Sloppy living can not only lead to physical ailments but also to a negative attitude.

5. I'm going to be joining a health club, I'm going to be going on a diet, and I'm going to be following my doctor's advice.

6. My warm-up includes stretches, pushups, and doing walking.

7. My workouts include playing basketball, climbing stairs, and jumping jacks.

8. Many people don't exercise enough because they think they don't have time and because of the softness of their couches.

9. Those who expect immediate results from exercise are going to be disappointed or they will be angry.

10. I took years to reach this condition, so I expect it will take months to change the condition significantly.

SENTENCE STYLE: 52e–h—Sentence Variety

Follow the directions in parentheses after each of the following sentences.

EXAMPLE:

An acid is a sour-tasting substance. Lemon juice is an acid. Acid often dissolves other materials. (Combine into one sentence.)

An acid, such as lemon juice, is a sour-tasting substance that often dissolves other materials.

a. John Polanyi, who won the Nobel Prize for his research in chemistry, is a campaigner for socially conscious science. (Rewrite as two sentences.)

b. The experiment succeeded. (Add an adjective.)

c. The experiment succeeded. (Add an adverb.)

d. The experiment succeeded. (Add an adverb clause.)

e. The experiment succeeded. (Add an adjective clause.)

1. Haemophilia is an inherited disease. It is caused by a deficiency or abnormality of one of the clotting factors. These factors are in the blood. Haemophiliacs can bleed to death from even small cuts or bruises. (Combine into one sentence.)

2. The eagle plummeted out of the clouds. (Invert the word order by placing the verb before the subject.)

3. The wind blew. (Add an adjective.)

4. The wind blew. (Add an adverb.)

5. The wind blew. (Add a prepositional phrase.)

6. The wind blew. (Add a participial phrase.)

7. The wind blew. (Add an absolute phrase.)

8. The wind blew. (Add an adverb phrase.)

9. The wind blew. (Add an adverb clause.)

10. The wind blew. (Add an adjective clause.)

WORDS: 54b—Choosing Exact Words

The first three lettered sentences and first five numbered sentences contain inappropriate denotations or connotations. The other sentences contain general or abstract phrases. Revise accordingly.

EXAMPLES:

famous.

Mahatma Gandhi is ~~notorious.~~ (denotation/connotation)

at 3:45 p.m.

Meet me ~~this afternoon.~~ (general/abstract)

a. My nephew's extremities need washing. (denotation/connotation)

b. The basketball player is lofty. (denotation/connotation)

c. Her perfume has a wonderful odour. (denotation/connotation)

d. I ate a meal. (general/abstract)

e. The cheeseburger cost a lot of money. (general/abstract)

1. My aunt ordered me to make myself at home. (denotation/connotation)

2. I buy my groceries at the boutique. (denotation/connotation)

3. The professor imparted to us that we'd have a quiz soon. (denotation/connotation)

4. I slyly guessed the last three questions on the quiz. (denotation/connotation)

5. Professor Krulicki eulogized me on my vocabulary. (denotation/connotation)

6. I read the book. (general/abstract)

7. We watched two hours of the dullest movie ever: *Holiday Slashers III*. (general/abstract)

8. I want to complete my education. (general/abstract)

9. Paul Moulin called for action on cities. (general/abstract)

10. Stephen Hopper supported spending programs. (general/abstract)

WORDS: 54d–g—Suitable Language, Figurative Language, Clichés, and Tone

Revise words with inappropriate impact in the following sentences if necessary.

EXAMPLE:

prison.

The gang members were threatened with fifteen years of ~~rehabilitation.~~

a.   Surprisingly, the actor known as "America's Sweetheart" was a Canadian, Mary Pickford.

b.   I think I'll flunk accounting.

c.   Alexander the Great had a cool idea when he decided to make Babylon his new capital.

d.   The door wouldn't close because the carpenters had inserted it at variance with the instructions.

e.   I've heard that the ambassador has been dissing our prime minister again.

1.   We ain't done.

2.   King Mark thought for sure that Tristan and Isolde had hooked up.

3.   Venus Williams plays tennis with the methodical grace and patience of a lioness hunting prey.

4.   If I don't get a handle on these math problems, I'll totally blow math class.

5.   The candidate misspoke herself.

6.   He's happy as a lark and smart as a whip.

7.   A person needs to be tough as nails to reach the top of the heap.

8.   After all is said and done, far be it from me at this point in time to disagree.

9.   He simply hasn't got the wherewithal to invest in my hedge fund, if you know what I mean.

10.   In bombing the town, the coalition forces caused collateral damage.

WORDS: 55—Using Inclusive Language

Revise sexist language in the following sentences.

EXAMPLE:

specialized
Operating a drill press is a ~~man-sized~~ job.

a. Ursula Franklin is a woman scientist.

b. The Charter gives every citizen the right to speak his mind.

c. The men in the room applauded.

d. All policemen should be honest.

e. Mike was a house husband: He cleaned, took care of the children, and cooked.

1. Before sending in the forms, a taxpayer should check his calculations.

2. Mr. Doe and his wife, Jane Doe, live in Frostbite Falls, Manitoba.

3. When a driver is stopped for a traffic violation, she should be polite to the policeman.

4. Polyester is a man-made material.

5. What country sent the first man into space?

6. An elementary school teacher has her hands full, since she works with so many giggling girls and rowdy boys.

7. Women who want to become better cooks should read this magazine.

8. Every night, the downtown office buildings are occupied by an army of cleaning ladies.

9. The common man doesn't understand the treaty.

10. Men need to have extensive training before they can qualify to become pilots.

WORDS: 56—Spelling

Correct misspelled words in the following sentences.

EXAMPLE:

sisters-in-law
My two ~~sister in laws~~ live in Corner Brook.

a. Our university employs two coaches for its lacrosse team.

b. That strategy has effected the team's sucess rate..

c. This is the forth year in five that the team has had a winning season.

d. We should complement the coaches on there success.

e. In the light of this record, though, the coachs probably won't altar much for next year.

1. Tornadoes occur relatively frequently on the Great Planes in late spring and in the summer.

2. They are often accompanied by rain, hail, and lightening.

3. Tornadoes themselves affect relatively small areas; there normally ten metres to less than two kilometers wide.

4. Buildings and trees hit by a tornado are often raised to the ground.

5. People have seen tornadoes move army tanks, farm combines, and railroad cars.

6. As in the movie *The Wizard of Oz*, in which a tornado picks up Dorothy's house, tornadoes have moved hole houses.

7. A tornado is able to brake nearly anything in its path, since its winds reach 500 km/h.

8. Buildings that are not tornado-proof seam to collapse like a house of cards.

9. During a few minutes, a thunderstorm that produces a tornado might let lose the same energy as a large atomic blast.

10. When human structures and tornadoes meat, the tornadoes normally win.

WORDS: 56a—Spelling Plurals

Correct misspelled words in the following sentences.

EXAMPLE:

coaches.

My brother and my sister are both ~~coachs~~.

a.   Carl prefers his french frys without ketchup.

b.   He was at two beachs yesterday.

c.   He wore a shirt with long sleeves, but he also wore swim trunks.

d.   He wore shoes, so his foots are fine.

e.   Carl is one of my brother-in-laws.

1.   Two mooses locked in mortal combat is an image that is hard to forget.

2.   The one criteria that interests me is the one that my professors all ignore.

3.   In this folder, I keep the syllabi for all my classes.

4.   We ate three bowles of rice.

5.   We saw a herd of elks when we were at the zoo.

6.   Henry VIII had many wifes in his lifetime.

7.   Did you rake the leafs?

8.   Potatos come from the great Inca civilization of the Andies.

9.   Warren wooed Jade with box's of clementines.

10. In death, we are all alumnuses of life, but we never return to the old alma mater for Homecoming Day.

WORDS: 56b–c—Adding Suffixes and Spelling *ie, ei* Words

Correct misspelled words in the following sentences.

EXAMPLE:

supersede
In my opinion, fast food will never ~~supercede~~ home-cooked food.

a. The teacher said that Sarah was logicaly inclined.

b. I beleive I will vote against the honourable member's motion.

c. Did you paint the cieling?

d. When did they begin requiring a jacket and tie in the restaurant?

e. That was the most forgetable movie I've ever seen.

1. The motorcycle cost eight thousand dollars.

2. My nieghbour bought it.

3. She will likly not ride it in the fields.

4. I find myself likeing to read more than I did when I was in high school.

5. I have a strong drive to succede.

6. Al droped all his English courses.

7. Has Al tryed the department's essay-writing clinic?

8. Statisticly, students who attend the clinic tend to succeed..

9. Preparing the breifing gave us a good deal of grief.

10. That was a wierd movie.

37

WORDS: 56d—Spelling Homonyms and Frequently Confused Words

Correct misspelled words in the following sentences.

EXAMPLE:

    too
I ate ~~to~~ many potato chips.

a. The bride and groom walked down the isle.

b. I except the invitation.

c. I'm intrigued by Freud's idea of the subconscience.

d. Have you seen the television program?

e. Often, a province's capitol is not the province's biggest city.

1. My mother is principle at an elementary school.

2. Who's hat is this?

3. Is it you're hat?

4. Was that you peaking through the blinds?

5. Spelling bees are my favourite passed times.

6. Did you see the lightening?

7. Queen Victoria reined even longer than Elizabeth I.

8. Everyone please precede into the waiting lounge.

9. I would like to by the chair buy next week.

10. Should I die my hair?

WORDS: 56d—Spelling Homonyms and Frequently Confused Words

Correct misspelled words in the following sentences.

EXAMPLE:

illusion.

The Wizard of Oz is a master of ~~allusion.~~

a.   I'm out of breathe after jogging.

b.   Cheese and milk are diary products.

c.   Fold the petition and place it carefully in an envelop.

d.   Ann lead the marching band yesterday.

e.   I dressed up as a witch for a costume party.

1.   Every Wednesday evening he is sure to be were he cannot be found.

2.   Due to unforeseen circumstances, I maybe late this evening.

3.   Hunger is still an every day experience for poor people around the world.

4.   I wish to respectively disagree.

5.   I prefer the later, rather than the former.

6.   The fable's morale is clear.

7.   I'm driving up the coast of Vancouver Island to see its most scenic sites.

8.   Did you chose wisely?

9.   This lever is a handy devise.

10.   Did your friend engage in elicit activity?

Add or delete commas in the following sentences if necessary.

EXAMPLE:

anger,
The seven deadly sins are ~~anger~~ covetousness (greed), envy, gluttony, lust, pride, and sloth.

a. Myopia or nearsightedness is a visual defect.

b. To myopic people distant objects appear blurred.

c. A myopic person's eyes focus light in front of the retina but a nonmyopic person's eyes focus light on the retina.

d. A person who wears glasses or contact lenses may be myopic.

e. Myopia therefore, is a visual defect that ordinarily can be corrected.

1. The word, *deadline* was first used in the mid-nineteenth century.

2. In a notorious prisoner of war camp guards could shoot prisoners who crossed a boundary line several metres inside the outer wall.

3. A deadline originally was a physical line not to be crossed but now, 150 years later it is a line in time not to be crossed.

4. "For truth there is no deadline" wrote Heywood Broun.

5. *The Nation* published Broun's article on December 30 1939.

6. Writers who can meet deadlines.

7. Millions of people took Thalidomide during the 1950s and 1960s didn't they?

8. Most of these people suffered no ill effects, but at least 10 000 women who took Thalidomide during their pregnancies gave birth to physically deformed but otherwise healthy babies.

9. The deformities included missing or stunted limbs such as hands at the elbows, two fingers instead of five and flippers rather than legs.

10. Gilla Kaplan MD discovered in 1989 how Thalidomide affects the immune system and realized that the drug might be useful in fighting a number of diseases.

PUNCTUATION AND MECHANICS: 57—Commas

Add or delete commas in the following sentences if necessary.

EXAMPLE:

160
Light heavyweight boxers weigh between ~~160,~~ and 175 pounds.

a. Although, Canada's area is 10 000 000 square kilometres, its population is only about 34 000 000 people.

b. Canada produces large quantities of wheat, and beef.

c. Much of Canada lies in the harsh, northern latitudes.

d. Copper, gold, nickel, and zinc, are some of the abundant minerals in Canada's reserves.

e. Winnipeg, Manitoba, is home to one of the best ballet companies in North America.

1. Miss Muffet sat on a tuffet, and ate curds and whey.

2. Miss Muffet apparently wanted to sit on the tuffet, but, a spider frightened her away.

3. During her subsequent trial for assault, Miss Muffet testified that, she returned to the tuffet with a can of Raid to retaliate against the spider which had sat down beside her.

4. Miss Muffet, who was little, sat on a tuffet.

5. Little, Miss Muffet sat on a tuffet.

6. The Barenaked Ladies, one of the biggest bands of the 1990s grew up together in Scarborough.

7. Does that refer to Scarborough Ontario on the east side of Toronto?

8. They are one of the rare bands, that can write music that is bouncy and simple but always interesting.

9. When the City of Toronto barred the Barenaked Ladies from playing a public concert, (their name was said to be offensive) thousands of fans wondered who on earth was in charge at city hall.

10. Many of their songs, including "If I Had a Million Dollars," "Jane," and "It's All Been Done" are perennial favourites.

PUNCTUATION AND MECHANICS: 57—Commas

Delete commas in the following sentences if necessary.

EXAMPLE:

The oak tree that I planted two years ago, is growing.

The oak tree that I planted two years ago is growing.

a.   Two expensive, unavoidable tasks await me.

b.   The first is to get a new, hard drive for my computer.

c.   The next, is to pay off my data plan, which got completely out of hand in just a few days following December 31, 2010.

d.   Doctors, who take the Hippocratic oath, pledge to do no harm.

e.   We drove 1200, kilometres on Friday.

1.   The crowd held their breath, intently.

2.   The, small restless crowd waited for the fireworks display.

3.   The display featured, many of the same fireworks used every year.

4.   A band named, Arcade Fire, travels with suitcases full of instruments of all kinds.

5.   Although, the professor talked about the next test, few students listened to him.

6.   I listened, and breezed through the test.

7.   I listened, crammed, and then paid attention, to the test instructions.

8.   I celebrated, because I got an A.

9.   Because I got an A, I treated my roommates to sushi.

10.   We celebrated, with a big order of sushi, rather than the usual pizza.

PUNCTUATION AND MECHANICS: 58—Semicolons

Revise the following sentences if necessary by adding or deleting semicolons, by substituting semicolons for other marks of punctuation, or by substituting other marks of punctuation for semicolons.

EXAMPLE:

today;
We biked 80 kilometres ~~today,~~ the workout was superb.

a. The committee included Ravi Diaram, the new accountant, Sarah Jarna, the coordinator of the advertising division, and Tracy Youngblood, the director of public relations.

b. I enjoy discussing trivia, especially about Canadian celebrities, and reading Canadian, American, and British poetry, nevertheless, I spend most of my spare time earning money to pay for tuition.

c. Susan Musgrave is a well-known poet, however, many people first heard about her when her husband, also a writer, was arrested for bank robbery.

d. Musgrave, who is from British Columbia, says she discovered that she was a "misfit" at an early age, her kindergarten teacher expelled her for laughing in class.

e. Musgrave amusingly gave one of her books the title *Great Musgrave*; this is the name of a tiny village in England.

1. The doctor's secretary told me, "If you have this examination without a referral; your provincial health plan may require you to pay for it."

2. The secretary said, "The doctor's appointment book is full today; we'll put you down for around lunch time tomorrow."

3. While waiting for my appointment, I flipped through three issues of *Maclean's,* checked my text messages, e-mail, and phone calls, and composed and revised the abstract for my physics report.

4. As I worked on the abstract for my report, my symptoms began to disappear; although I stayed until the doctor was ready to see me.

5. It was a good thing that I stayed; for the doctor diagnosed a condition that could have become worse if left untreated.

6. Shakespeare wrote *Antony and Cleopatra*; *As You Like It*; *Hamlet*; *Julius Caesar*, *King Lear*, and *Macbeth*.

7. Shakespeare was born in Stratford-on-Avon, however, he spent most of his career in London.

8. He worked as an actor; playwright; and manager of the Globe Theatre.

9. He spent his retirement back in Stratford; where he died in 1616.

10. The *First Folio*; the earliest collected edition of his plays; was published in 1623.

PUNCTUATION AND MECHANICS: 59—Colons

Revise the following sentences if necessary by adding or deleting colons, by substituting colons for other marks of punctuation, or by substituting other marks of punctuation for colons.

EXAMPLE:

        sure: The
Of this I am ~~sure, the~~ car will give you trouble within three months.

a. Imitating the title of Stephen W. Hawking's book *A Brief History of Time: From the Big Bang to Black Holes*, my brother called his paper *A Brief History of My Time in the Chemistry Lab: From Unknown Chemicals to Unknown Chemicals.*

b. Take the 7 05 commuter train to Union Station.

c. Unless there is further political reform, I can already predict the result, another minority government.

d. Governments in Canada are under constant pressure to: promote national unity, fund health care adequately, and assert Canada's presence in the United Nations.

e. The original Greek text of John 1,1 has never been adequately translated.

1. Canadians evaluate their governments in a number of areas, including: promotion of national unity, support for health care, and assertion of Canada's presence in the United Nations.

2. I will never forget the first time I tried to ski: I fell in the middle of the slope and struggled for twenty minutes to get up.

3. The Queen of Hearts, in Lewis Carroll's *Alice's Adventures in Wonderland*, has an easy but gruesome answer whenever anyone bothers her, "Off with her head! Off with his head!"

4. As you will recall: Yesterday's subject was the fine art of punctuating a sentence.

5. One of hockey's historic arenas is the former home of the Montreal Canadiens; the Forum.

6. In Richard Brinsley Sheridan's play *The Rivals*, Mrs. Malaprop says: "He is the very *pineapple* of politeness."

7. She means: *pinnacle.*

8. A malapropism today is: a word misused as Mrs. Malaprop might have used it.

9.   When my roommate and I went to see *The Rivals*: we laughed louder than the other people in the audience.

10.   They must have been puzzled regarding: the reason for our hilarity.

PUNCTUATION AND MECHANICS: 58–59—Semicolons and Colons

Revise the following sentences if necessary by adding or deleting semicolons or colons, by substituting semicolons or colons for other marks of punctuation, or by substituting other marks of punctuation for semicolons or colons.

EXAMPLE:

                                    including the
The Acropolis is the site of famous ruins, ~~including: The~~ Parthenon.

a. Although David Cronenberg appears on many lists of the world's greatest film directors; early in his career he directed advertisements and short features for television.

b. The advertisements included: spots for Ontario Hydro, a running shoe company, and even a brand of chocolate bar.

c. Cronenberg's films have seldom attracted mainstream audiences, nevertheless, *A History of Violence* earned him popular success and an armful of awards.

d. Atom Egoyan has made a long list of acclaimed dramatic films, including: *The Sweet Hereafter, The Adjuster, Speaking Parts, Exotica,* and *Ararat.*

e. Egoyan has also staged an opera: Richard Strauss's *Salome.*

1. Body language includes: gestures and eye contact.

2. The North American gesture for "okay" involves forming a circle with the forefinger and thumb, this gesture means: "zero" in France.

3. The North American gesture for "okay" has various meanings in other cultures, such as: "zero" in France, "money" in Japan, and a vulgarity in Brazil.

4. Business people in foreign countries need to understand that body language has various meanings depending on culture, otherwise, they may offend prospective customers.

5. Although looking someone in the eye means honesty in Canada and the United States; in most Asian and Latin American countries, it might mean aggression or ill breeding.

6. Asian business people tend to prefer: brief or no handshakes, sitting side by side during negotiations, and long negotiations.

7. In contrast to business people in the Middle East, who usually stand less than one metre apart when talking; business people in Canada and the United States usually stand nearly two metres apart.

8. One submission wanted the biology text to begin by quoting Genesis 1,1.

9. Math majors outnumbered other science majors in the calculus class by 2-1.

10. The marathon runner crossed the finish line in 3:15:10.

PUNCTUATION AND MECHANICS: 60—Apostrophes

Add or delete apostrophes in the following sentences if necessary. Word changes may be necessary, as in the example.

EXAMPLE:

        whose
My roommate, ~~who's~~ talents do not include cooking, can barely boil water.

a.   Nunavuts area is two million square kilometres.

b.   Its population is equivalent to that of a small city.

c.   As the newest territory in Canada's north, Nunavut has attracted the attention of many Canadians'.

d.   It's easy to imagine all the challenges facing this territorys leaders.

e.   The government of Nunavut is responsible to all of it's people, but it has a special duty to protect the Inuit people's lands and culture.

1.   Ontario's official flower is the trillium, but whats Nunavut's?

2.   No ones going to believe that.

3.   How many *us* appear in *Iqaluit*?

4.   Gilbert's and Sullivan's operettas include *Patience, H.M.S. Pinafore,* and *The Mikado.*

5.   Gilbert and Sullivan wrote their operetta's in the late 1800s'.

6.   The music is difficult, so only experienced singers' can sing the lead roles.

7.   Many years ago I promised to take Leila to a performance of *Patience,* if she were patient enough to wait for one to be staged on a date that had four 2s.

8.   To my delight and also her's, my silly promise eventually came due on March 22, 2002.

9.   We joined the crowd at the door's of our cities' new opera house.

10.   As expected, during intermission the line outside the ladies' room was nearly endless, while no one had to wait long to get into the mens' room.

49

PUNCTUATION AND MECHANICS: 61—Quotation Marks

Add or delete quotation marks and revise other punctuation in the following sentences if necessary. Also revise any tired or inappropriate language enclosed in quotation marks in the following sentences.

EXAMPLE:

What did Mackenzie King mean when he said that Canada would have

conscription"?

"conscription if necessary, but not necessarily ~~conscription?"~~

a. I am reading a short story by Robertson Davies, The Charlottetown Banquet."

b. An item on Feist's website reads: "We are beyond pleased to report that on April 29, a flash mob of 300 dancers infiltrated the public concourse of the Eaton Centre, Toronto, with a mass dance to Feist's "Feel It All" remix by Escort".

c. Many people confuse lie and lay.

d. The music programmer told me "This group's "new" sound comes from sampling old material from its own bestselling album."

e. Thomas Gray's poem "Elegy Written in a Country Churchyard" contains the line "The paths of glory lead but to the grave."

1. In the book "Stolen Continents", Ronald Wright says, "In the summer of 1990, the Iroquois were suddenly reborn in white consciousness when Canadian front pages were filled for three months by what came to be known as the Oka Crisis or Mohawk Revolt."

2. Wright believes that the Iroquois should never have disappeared from what he calls white consciousness."

3. In "Whom says so?" in *The Nation*, June 8, 1985, Calvin Trillin writes. 'As far as I'm concerned, "whom" is a word that was invented to make everyone sound like a butler'.

4. Trembling, Dante asked himself, "Did the instructions above that door really begin with the words "Abandon hope"?

5. "Dante," said Virgil, I am here to guide you on your journey."

6. I like the Latin proverb *Ars longa, vita brevis* (life is short, art is long").

7. Chaucer translated the proverb as The life so short, the art so long to learn.

8. Have you read Susan Musgrave's poem "Arctic Poppies?"

9. Seth thinks that "the Bottles" will be "the second coming" of the Beatles, but Jo expects the group to be just "a flash in the pan."

10. "Defamation" is a false and malicious statement, one communicated to others, that injures a person's reputation; "defamation" in writing is "libel."

PUNCTUATION AND MECHANICS: 62—Periods, Question Marks, and Exclamation Marks

Correct end punctuation in the following sentences if necessary.

EXAMPLE:

We wondered if we would make it to the airport on time?.
⌃

a. In 1968 Pierre Trudeau proclaimed his intention to make Canada a "just society"

b. Did some people hear in this plan an echo of US president Lyndon Johnson's "great society"?

c. I asked my professor if this was true?

d. She confirmed my idea, but unfortunately(!), she suggested that I analyze the differences between the two slogans in my mid-term paper.

e. How do you think I should approach that. From the point of view of individual personality? national traditions? social problems, linguistic and racial issues?

1. Tara is moving into a quiet (?) apartment next to a ramp onto the Trans-Canada Highway.

2. "Listen, everybody. I mean now."

3. "I'm melting," wailed the Wicked Witch of the West. "I'm melting."

4. The director cried out, "Start shooting already."

5. The camera crew asked if David Cronenberg had cried out "Start shooting already"?

6. Did the actor who was reaching for his gun hear David Cronenberg cry out "Start shooting already?"

7. People of earth, lay down your weapons and prepare to be conquered.

8. We asked the invaders if earth conquest meant the end of professional sport as we knew it?

9. Of all the provinces, only Prince Edward Island (!) resisted the extraterrestrial invaders.

10. Which provinces welcomed them.

PUNCTUATION AND MECHANICS: 63—Other Punctuation Marks

Add or delete punctuation marks in the following sentences if necessary.

EXAMPLE:

Leonard Cohen, Mordecai Richler, and David Fennario are all English-speakers from Montreal, but these three (3) writers could hardly be more different.

a.   Pandora opened the box that Zeus had given her—so the story goes—and let loose all the evils and miseries that now afflict humanity.

b.   Some bacteria those that live in the digestive tract and aid digestion, for example are beneficial to humans.

c.   Regrettably, we cannot endorse an annual report containing erroneous statements such as "Our profits for this fiscal year amounted to $20 trillion (sic!), a figure we were hoping to improve on."

d.   In her poem "Chahinkapa Zoo," Louise Erdrich writes about the frustration wild animals in zoos must feel (but can animals really feel frustration); the poem begins, "It is spring. Even here / The bears emerge from poured caverns. / Already their cubs have been devoured / by the feather-footed lynx caged next door."

e.   Erdrich's zoo is a nasty place in which the bears' "cubs have been devoured by the lynx caged next door."

1.   They love Italian food, minestrone soup, pasta, and grated hard cheese.

2.   Richard Burton the writer and explorer, not the actor lived in the nineteenth century.

3.   The agenda for the Edmonton Arts and Letters Alliance meeting includes 1 considering whether we should rent a new studio, 2 recruiting new members, and 3, considering whether we should decorate our premises with new works of art.

4.   The Edmonton Arts and Letters Alliance would like to place an order for (six) 6 paintings by Lawren Harris.

5.   This circuit on the computer is hard-wired, built to do a specific job, so it needs no program to function properly.

6. Although some fears appear to be hard-wired into some animal brains, (falling, for example), we do not understand the brain well enough to say conclusively that it functions exactly like a computer.

7. Rebuilding the pier (waves destroyed most of the original.) took two months.

8. Only about 1:10 of the original pier was left standing.

9. The humourist Stephen Leacock, who was also an economist, wrote (perhaps he was speaking for both professions), "To dig out gold in North Ontario and dig it in, in Tennessee, is on the face of it idiocy."

10. Stephen Leacock wrote, "To dig out gold in North Ontario and dig it in, in Tennessee (the location of Fort Knox), is on the face of it idiocy."

PUNCTUATION AND MECHANICS: 64—Hyphens

Revise the hyphens in the following sentences if necessary.

EXAMPLE:

The final test will be all inclusive.

The final test will be all-inclusive.

a.   The Cozmic Gear Company's unionized employees presented a petition for redress of the discrimination practised against newly hired cog fitters.

b.   "Self love" is one way to translate the French expression *amour propre*.

c.   Each of the graduated bowls that make a glass harmonica will produce a belllike tone of a particular pitch when you press your finger to its moistened rim.

d.   The play director asked all cast members to redress for a group picture.

e.   The more-expensive coat is the better-looking coat.

1.   A short tempered referee officiated at our hockey game.

2.   One half of our team's goals were scored by a reserve defence player.

3.   The other team's ill fated goalie left the game before the end of the first period.

4.   A period in our old timer hockey league doesn't last a full-twenty minutes.

5.   The new over-pass allows trucks one-metre's clearance.

6.   The Milky Way is 100 000 light years in diameter.

7.   Premier elect Robichaud spoke to us.

8.   Anti-intellectual students will not enjoy Ms. Smith's class.

9.   A toaster running for one hour will normally use one kilowatt hour of electricity.

10. The Sharmas are a happily-married couple.

PUNCTUATION AND MECHANICS: 65—Capitals

Add or delete capitals in the following sentences if necessary.

EXAMPLE:

        Like
Ursula Franklin has written, "~~like~~ democracy, technology is a multifaceted entity. It includes activities as well as a body of knowledge, structures as well as the act of structuring."

a.   Ursula Franklin has been a Research Scientist, a university Professor, and an antiwar activist.

b.   Before she came to Canada, Franklin had been a victim of Nazi persecution.

c.   After leaving her research position, Franklin (1) Became the first female professor in her university department, (2) Worked on the application of physics and chemistry to archaeology, and (3) Joined the Royal Society of Canada.

d.   In 2002, the United nations association in Canada awarded her the Pearson peace Medal.

e.   Franklin has said that "In the post–September 11 world, it is doubly important to explore the means of peace and cooperation because in the face of violence, one forgets so easily the solutions . . . that were achieved without war."

1.   If threatened, a horned toad has a unique defence: It squirts blood at its adversaries from a place near its eyes.

2.   In addition to the spines on their bodies, horned toads have four forms of defence: (1) Blending into the environment, (2) Inflating to appear larger, (3) Running away, and (4) Squirting blood.

3.   "Horned toads," the biology professor explained, "Are actually lizards, not toads."

4.   Horned toads are native to the band of land extending from the southern part of British Columbia to Northern Guatemala.

5.   Horned toads, like other reptiles, are Ectotherms—their body temperature rises and falls with the temperature of their environment.

6.   Isaac Brock was a General in the War of 1812.

7.   Brock died at the battle of Queenston Heights in upper Canada.

8.   Today Brock may be better known for the University that bears his name.

9. Unflattering nicknames given to John A. Macdonald include "Old tomorrow" and "fox populi."

10. "Until that road is built to British Columbia and the pacific," Macdonald said about the Canadian Pacific railway, Canada would remain "A mere geographical expression."

PUNCTUATION AND MECHANICS: 66—Italics (Underlining)

Either add or remove italics or quotation marks in the following sentences if necessary.

EXAMPLE:

It is not hard to find *pierogies* in Winnipeg.

It is not hard to find pierogies in Winnipeg.

a. In his book *Marginalia*, Mark Kingwell mentions that his life in Toronto has revolved around the neighbourhood commonly known as "the Annex."

b. We flew in a *Dash 8* commuter jet named *The City of Ottawa*.

c. The decreases in our foreign-aid budget have left many Canadians *deeply* disappointed.

d. Canada's oldest weekly news magazine is "Maclean's."

e. Leonard Cohen's *Suzanne* is both a poem and a song.

1. Margaret Atwood's early novel "Surfacing" helped establish her reputation as a writer of prose fiction.

2. Tom Thomson's painting "The West Wind" is reproduced in the article on Thomson in "The Canadian Encyclopedia."

3. Irving Layton wrote a short poem with the title Misunderstanding.

4. Canada's first scientific satellite was named *Alouette I*.

5. Did audiences agree with film critics about Atom Egoyan's Chloe?

6. An interesting version of Neil Young's "Helpless" appears on the album "Hymns of the 49th Parallel."

7. Do you like *sushi*?

8. I nearly wrote that the singer "brought the house down," but I didn't—I wanted to avoid using a *cliché*.

9. Do you read the Calgary Herald?

10. The *Three Tenors* tried our patience with endless encores of one number from Puccini's opera *Turandot*.

PUNCTUATION AND MECHANICS: 67—Abbreviations

Revise the abbreviations and punctuation marks in the following sentences if necessary.

EXAMPLE:

The concert will begin at 7:30 p.m..

The concert will begin at 7:30 p.m.

a. While discussing the pessimism so pervasive in the fourteenth century (1300–1399 AD), Barbara Tuchman writes in her book *A Distant Mirror*, "Death is not treated poetically as the soul's flight to reunion with God; it is a skeleton grinning at the vanity of life."

b. The university hopes to increase its endowment fund to $250 million.

c. Dr. Bette Stephenson, MD, gave up her medical practice to run for the provincial legislature.

d. Canada participated in the Boer War, the First World War, etc., but not in the 2003 invasion of Iraq.

e. The application was sent to 2200 Wascana Rd., in Saskatoon.

1. My job starts at 8:30 A.M.

2. Julius Caesar introduced the Julian calendar in Rome in BC 46.

3. A yard equals 36 in.

4. Why go for a skiing holiday in the US when you can drive to Mont Tremblant?

5. PM John Turner lost power at the first opportunity.

6. Dr. Richard Rodriguez, PhD, published *Days of Obligation* in 1993.

7. Look for live streaming and archived concerts on C.B.C.'s Radio 3 site.

8. St. John's, Nfld., has many distinctive wooden bldgs.

9. Archaeologists give the measurements of the artifacts they discover in cm.

10. Please send the bill to Oak St. NW, Graniteville, which, as you know, is in ON.

PUNCTUATION AND MECHANICS: 68—Numbers

Revise numbers in the following sentences if necessary.

EXAMPLE:

1998 was a good year.

Nineteen ninety-eight was a good year.

a. Bart Simpson and his family first appeared on TV on April nineteenth, 1987.

b. World War II ended in Europe on May 8, 1945.

c. Uranium's melting point is 1132°C, and its boiling point is three thousand eight hundred and eighteen degrees C.

d. During my shift, I received thirty five 911 calls.

e. The department office opens at 9 o'clock every weekday morning.

1. You'll find Table C on page thirty-six.

2. She wrote her 3 best novels in a ten-year period.

3. I live at fifteen Elm Street.

4. We'll meet at 3 o'clock.

5. We'll meet at 3 in the afternoon.

6. I've written 3 quarters of my paper.

7. 1976 is the year in which Martha Wainwright was born.

8. A straight flush is ranked above four of a kind in poker.

9. A centimetre is 1/one-hundredth the length of a metre.

10. I listen to the radio station located at ninety-three point three FM.

TIPS FOR MULTILINGUAL WRITERS: 69a—Count and Noncount Nouns

Underline count nouns once and noncount nouns twice in the following sentences.

EXAMPLE:

Oxygen is a gas.

a. Hot air rises.

b. Hot air balloons rise.

c. I packed my clothing in the suitcase.

d. I packed my equipment in the bag.

e. Do you speak French?

1. Do you live in an apartment?

2. Did you listen to the radio?

3. Chemistry is my major.

4. My major is chemistry.

5. I counted the items.

6. She counted her change.

7. She bought fifteen litres of gasoline.

8. Did you bring your luggage?

9. I am attending classes to learn something.

10. Do you know if Andra has a new avatar?

TIPS FOR MULTILINGUAL WRITERS: 69a, 42a–c, 43a—Singulars and Plurals

Change the verbs in the following sentences from singular to plural or from plural to singular if necessary.

EXAMPLE:

      is
Chess ~~are~~ a challenging game.

a.   My birthday are two days away.

b.   Ice are cold.

c.   The snows this winter were heavier but less frequent than last winter.

d.   My shoes is wet.

e.   Gasoline are expensive in Nunavut.

1.   Rice are a staple of many people's diet.

2.   Chinese are a language spoken by two of my friends.

3.   Eggs is used in many baked goods.

4.   The smog are particularly bad today.

5.   My clothing are in my suitcase.

6.   Comparative politics are my major.

7.   The heat have been unbearable this month.

8.   Before the Internet, television were more popular with teenagers.

9.   Aluminum are a metal.

10.   The coffee has double cream and double sugar.

TIPS FOR MULTILINGUAL WRITERS: 69b—Singulars and Plurals

Add or delete determiners in the following sentences if necessary.

EXAMPLE:

Are there ~~the~~ computer terminals in this room?

a.   Does she live in big house on corner?

b.   I live in apartment near here.

c.   The tomatoes are tasty in salads.

d.   This rice tastes good.

e.   He has a few sheets of a paper.

1.   The university has built new library.

2.   One of books for this course was very expensive.

3.   Did you buy the another high-tech water bottle?

4.   Her handheld device is new.

5.   Our bicycles are parked on sidewalk.

6.   Countryside is worth exploring when you study at Trent.

7.   She has the curly hair.

8.   Did your performance get lot of applause?

9.   We saw first movie.

10. Students who succeed take a pride in their schoolwork.

TIPS FOR MULTILINGUAL WRITERS: 70—Articles

Add or delete articles in the following sentences if necessary.

EXAMPLE:

```
                       an               the
The teacher brought  umbrella into  classroom.
                   ^       .      ^
```

a. It was a honour to receive an award.

b. Beaver, our national animal, is easy to find in Canada, although the lion, which is United Kingdom's national animal, is rarely seen there.

c. My dream is to have a chalet on the Lake Louise.

d. The cats are the animals that many people keep as pets.

e. Have you noticed that the Harpers and the Ignatieffs never show up at the same barbecue?

1. I sat on cold, metal chair.

2. I took advantage of an one-time-only offer on blue jeans.

3. Clouds are covering the sun.

4. The robins are migratory birds.

5. Bookshelf in my office is made of particle board.

6. I accidentally broke the bookshelf, so I bought new one.

7. My father planted the onions in his garden last week. We will eat the onions in a couple of months.

8. Before the arrival of the European explorers, Incas created a great civilization in South America.

9. The serenity is a good state of mind to achieve.

10. I would like to work for CBC.

TIPS FOR MULTILINGUAL WRITERS: 71—Word Order

Cross out misplaced words in the following sentences. Then mark a caret (^) to show where each word belongs, and write the word in above the caret.

EXAMPLE:

        wear
Should ~~wear~~ I   my red big coat?
        ^

a.   Will Sasha to the concert take Anastasia?

b.   Are my blue new slacks in the closet?

c.   Yesterday, I bought the three last tickets for the concert.

d.   Never we've heard this band before.

e.   I'm very excited about attending the concert.

1.   How did you the concert like?

2.   Why did you walk out of the concert?

3.   She asked me why did I walk out of that concert.

4.   Sasha did last night take Anastasia to the concert?

5.   The band's first song into the crowded auditorium blasted out.

6.   After the concert, we stopped at the new little restaurant on Elm Street.

7.   I ate incredibly a big cheeseburger.

8.   I had eaten two sandwiches and a red big apple only four hours earlier.

9.   I eat occasionally too much.

10.   She says that she overeats never.

TIPS FOR MULTILINGUAL WRITERS: 71b–c, 45—Adjectives and Adverbs

Underline adjectives once and adverbs twice in the following sentences.

EXAMPLE:

The big dog ran rapidly.

a.   I quickly ate the two eggs.

b.   I drank orange juice first, and then I ate two eggs.

c.   He devoured the fresh eggs rapidly.

d.   The yolks of these free-range eggs are bright yellow.

e.   We never eat raw eggs.

1.   The first ticket agent will be with you shortly.

2.   Did she say she'd be with us soon?

3.   We want to take a short trip tomorrow.

4.   My two friends have never been to Banff.

5.   They have heard that it's extremely beautiful.

6.   Sometimes I wonder if I need such an expensive car.

7.   I would gladly return the defective microwave if I could do so.

8.   Jim Carrey twice appeared in roles well below his talent level.

9.   He seldom finds screenwriters who fully use his great talents.

10. I don't have time to read this long book.

TIPS FOR MULTILINGUAL WRITERS: 72—Prepositions

Substitute a correct preposition for any preposition used incorrectly in the following sentences. Then delete any misplaced preposition, reinserting it in the correct position.

EXAMPLE:

on
When we meet ~~at~~ Saturday, I will introduce you to my parents.

a. We should meet our friends in a few minutes.

b. We'll meet Mario and Sidney in the hockey game.

c. Before we go in, we'll check our tickets for.

d. We need to get the bus off.

e. Look out for vehicles when we run the street across.

1. I'll have a birthday on a couple of weeks.

2. I'll have a party at the evening in my birthday.

3. I'll have the party at my apartment.

4. My apartment is in the brick building in the corner of Oak Drive and King Street.

5. I need to figure which games we'll play at the party out.

6. Will you help me call our friends on the West Coast up to find out if they will be able to attend?

7. I'll speak half of them with, and you can speak the other half of them with.

8. I've made a list so we won't leave out any of our friends.

9. We should go the list over one last time to make sure we didn't omit anybody.

10. Should we look renting a movie into for the party?

TIPS FOR MULTILINGUAL WRITERS: 73—Gerunds and Infinitives

Underline gerunds once and infinitives twice in the following sentences.

EXAMPLE:

Shall we go to see a movie?

a. We like to play cards after lunch.

b. We particularly enjoy playing bridge.

c. Do you promise to play bridge sometime?

d. We plan to play cards again on Friday.

e. We will try to play for an hour.

1. The battery in my smartphone seems to need replacing.

2. I'd seriously think of buying a new smartphone if my carrier had the latest ones in stock.

3. Don't you want to try the new operating system first?

4. When I was buying my phone last year, I knew not to rush into a decision.

5. Maybe we can go to the website to look at the specifications of the new models.

6. Lawrence has considered driving to Saskatoon.

7. Please let me buy you another cappuccino.

8. I would like to purchase you another expensive coffee.

9. I fail to understand your refusal.

10. I suggest keeping the possibility open for the time being.

TIPS FOR MULTILINGUAL WRITERS: 73—Gerunds and Infinitives

Change gerunds to infinitives or infinitives to gerunds in the following sentences if necessary.

EXAMPLE:

    playing
I enjoy ~~to play~~ basketball.

a.   Nicole cannot help to hate mosquitoes.

b.   As for me, I refuse being bothered by them.

c.   Why should I be unable tolerating such tiny insects?

d.   Nicole, however, won't risk to go outside on lovely summer evenings.

e.   She just can't seem to agree putting on full-body mosquito netting as I do.

1.   The boy began to cry and screaming.

2.   We tried wiping the tears and to talk to the child.

3.   The boy wanted going to the theatre where *Avatar* was playing.

4.   The boy's older sister appeared and arranged taking him that afternoon.

5.   Let me drive you to the nearest bus stop.

6.   Will you please help me figuring out the bus connections to the theatre?

7.   Do you recommend to take the 12-A bus to Third Avenue?

8.   I recall to take this bus recently.

9.   I promise buying a big bag of popcorn.

10.   Should we plan leaving at 3:30?

TIPS FOR MULTILINGUAL WRITERS: 74—Modal Auxiliary Verbs

Follow the directions in parentheses when revising the verb(s) in the following sentences.

EXAMPLE:

can
I shut the door. (present ability)
^

a. I work in the kitchen. (present ability)

b. I work in the kitchen. (present negative ability)

c. I work in the kitchen. (future advisability)

d. I work in the kitchen. (present preference)

e. I work in the kitchen. (past habit)

1. I grill the salmon. (future necessity)

2. I grill the salmon. (past advisability)

3. I grill the salmon. (present advisability)

4. I grill the salmon. (good advice)

5. I grill the salmon. (possibility)

6. I live in Nova Scotia. (past possibility)

7. I live in Nova Scotia. (present preference)

8. I live in Nova Scotia. (past preference)

9. I live in Nova Scotia. (past plan)

10. I live in Nova Scotia. (past habit)

REVIEW 1

Revise the following sentences at the level of sentences and words if necessary.

EXAMPLE:

      The   pitched

~~In fact, the~~ catcher ~~performed the action of pitching~~ batting practice.

a.   A bartender is a person who has a tendency to make cocktails.

b.   After the track meet, the winners received their medals.

c.   Even though her name is Emma, therefore she prefers to use the name Amina.

d.   The lion is an animal well designed for stalking, for chasing, and to overpower its prey.

e.   The elephant fluted in triumph when it defeated its opponent.

1.   At the present time, a plan exists to combat global warming.

2.   The plan reflects the urgent need to stop global warming.

3.   Manitoba's capital is Winnipeg, and the capital of New Brunswick is Fredericton.

4.   We left at the crack of dawn, so we could make the trip in one day.

5.   Prime Minister Chrétien and his wife Aline enjoyed their collection of Inuit sculpture.

6.   The average voter thinks his MP should be responsive to his concerns.

7.   Seiji Ozawa, who conducted the Toronto Symphony in the 1960s, was notorious for promoting modern classical music.

8.   Pinchas Zukerman conducted not only in the United States, but also he conducted in Canada.

9.   Scenic Quebec City still has its centuries old defensive walls. Quebec City was chosen for that reason as a UNESCO World Heritage Sight.

10.   Above the St. Lawrence river rise the stone ramparts and towers of the old city. Within these stone ramparts and these towers lies an old city of winding cobblestone streets and historic buildings.

REVIEW 2

Revise the following sentences if necessary.

EXAMPLE:

       led
New evidence ~~lead~~ the RCMP to open a file on the suspect last week.

a.   After the mixture boil for five minutes, it cool in the test tube.

b.   If everyone in the country went shopping for a new car tomorrow, would they generally buy or lease?

c.   The batter striked out, and in the blink of an eye the catcher through the ball to first base.

d.   The reason I got lost is because I was unfamiliar with the neighbourhood.

e.   Since he likes to ring doorbells, he started selling door-to-door.

1.   She speaking Spanish to her friends.

2.   Read the entire novel before you chose a passage to examine in your essay.

3.   I'll only pass you the book if you say "Please."

4.   The technical team inputted all the data for us, we broadcasted it the next day.

5.   Every mosquito and deer tick in this part of the province is a potential health hazard because their bite can spread disease.

6.   With discipline and patience, as well as a talent for the big shot, brought Sandra Schmirler's rink the curling championship.

7.   Her team always played very good.

8.   The reason this sandwich is less tasty is because it was made without butter.

9.   I like this sandwich better than the other sandwiches on the tray it was made with butter and mayonnaise.

10.   The sandwich with butter and mayonnaise is the most fattening sandwich on the tray.

REVIEW 3: Multilingual Writers

Revise the following sentences if necessary.

EXAMPLE:

                     tomorrow.

I should go to class ~~yesterday.~~

a.   Jann has just scheduled her major two next concert appearances.

b.   I have not listened her new album yet.

c.   Does she play the piano on any of her songs?

d.   I am thinking to take piano lessons soon.

e.   I can afford them because I have little money saved to hire a piano teacher.

1.   One of the most important innovations of our times are the rise of social networking sites.

2.   These sites let people anywhere share the current events, cultural events, and especially the personal information of all kinds.

3.   The main problem with these sites are that they put out too much personal information.

4.   Another problem may be the mass of data with which consumers of information are flooded.

5.   It can be hard to keep up all this information with.

6.   I enjoy to surf the Internet. Didn't you?

7.   You should visit my blog if you want to help me for our English course compile a list of useful websites.

8.   Last night I rather was working on my physics problem set.

9.   Rice sounds like a good idea for dinner.

10.   Should we flavour the rice with the curry?

REVIEW 4

Revise punctuation in the following sentences if necessary.

EXAMPLE:

that?”
“Did you see ~~that?”,~~ asked the surprised lifeguard.

a. Several famous boxers have taken the nickname Sugar Ray.

b. *Brillig* is a nonsense word that was coined by Lewis Carroll.

c. Chlorophyll makes plants green.

d. The exam is scheduled for 2.45.

e. The National Gallery, which operates under the 1990 Museums Act, is required to: develop, maintain, and make known Canadian Art.

1. According to a study published in 1980 in *Public Health Reports*: The survival rate for people who were recovering from heart attacks and who owned pets was higher than the survival rate for people without pets.

2. The study, whose findings were confirmed in 2008, seems to show that having a pet helps a person recover from a heart attack.

3. The mortality rate for people owning pets’ was about 1/3 that of the people who did not own pets.

4. One possible explanation is that: the pets helped their owners relax.

5. Computer literacy, in addition to familiarity with various handheld electronic devices, is typical of students, in colleges and universities, today.

6. The Internet, and the cell phone, have changed the way people interact, especially young people.

7. For example sending text messages on handheld devices quickly became wildly popular.

8. January 1, 2001 was on a Monday.

9. Astronomy is a scientific study: astrology, on the other hand, is not.

10. The month of March is named after the planet “Mars.”

REVIEW 5

Revise the following sentences if necessary.

EXAMPLE:

Ten-tonne
~~10-tonne~~ canaries say, "Here kitty, here kitty."

a. Compare the search results with "Google" and "Yahoo."

b. The bare walked back and forth all day long in its cage.

c. A well balanced diet includes foods from all the major food groups.

d. When Little Red Riding Hood comments on her grandmother's big tooths, the wolf (who is disguised as the grandmother) replies, "The better to eat you with!"

e. Nunavut is a territory; it is not a province.

1. The *Bluenose* is the name of the prize winning sailing ship pictured on the dime.

2. At one time, many European nations celebrated the new-year on or soon after Mar. 21.

3. Wilderness camping develops self reliance.

4. This is the best-fitting pair of shoes I have ever worn.

5. This pair costs only one half of what my other pair cost.

6. I road down the highway in a big grey Lexus.

7. He drove South on Queen Street.

8. Pro development city councillors hold the balance of power.

9. The speed limit is twenty five kilometres per hour.

10. Our class staged a production of "White Biting Dog" by playwright Judith Thompson.

75

Answers to Lettered Exercises

41b—Identifying Pronouns

a. Give <u>it</u> to <u>me</u>.

b. Give the ball to <u>me</u>.

c. Would <u>anybody</u> like to help <u>me</u> eat the pizza?

d. <u>This</u> is Jordan's running shoe.

e. Please return the shoe to Jordan. [Note: The unspoken pronoun *you* is often considered to be the subject of an imperative sentence; see 42f.]

41j—Subjects and Predicates   [Subject   Verb]

a. The <u>visitors</u> <u>said</u> goodbye.

b. <u>They</u> <u>stood</u> for a long time in the doorway.

c. <u>They</u> <u>seemed</u> sad about leaving.

d. The longer <u>they</u> <u>stayed</u>, the sadder <u>I</u> <u>became</u>.

e. <u>I</u> <u>was</u> tired, and <u>I</u> <u>wanted</u> them to leave.

42a—Transitive and Intransitive Verbs   [Transitive   Intransitive]

a. Jane <u>talked</u> slowly today.

b. She <u>spoke</u> too rapidly when she <u>gave</u> her speech yesterday.

c. The professor <u>leaned</u> forward and <u>listened</u> yesterday.

d. I <u>am</u> happy that she <u>spoke</u> slowly.

e. When I <u>give</u> speeches, I <u>speak</u> slowly.

42b—Regular and Irregular Verbs

a. Correct.

b. Have you ever dived off the high board?

c. I was a little shaken up by the experience.

d. Until recently, I would have sunk in water over my head.

e. I have grown stronger as a swimmer in recent weeks.

42b–c—Main and Auxiliary Verbs   [Main   Auxiliary]

a. It <u>is</u> <u>claimed</u> that the first snowboard <u>was</u> a cafeteria food tray that a mischievous student <u>swiped</u>.

b. By 1980, professional snowboards <u>were being manufactured</u>.

c. The Olympics <u>admitted</u> snowboarding as an official event in 1998.

d. The first gold medal <u>was awarded</u> to Ross Rebagliati, who <u>failed</u> a drug test just minutes afterward.

e.   Rebagliati would have lost his medal if Canadian officials had not noticed the absence of any Olympic ban against that particular drug.

42b, 42d—Irregular Verbs Including *lie* and *lay*

a.   Has Tera Van Beilen swum in her event yet?

b.   Correct.

c.   After a hard practice, the junior team lay down in an exhausted heap.

d.   Canada has become a force in swimming in the Youth Olympics.

e.   Rachel Nicol from Lethbridge fought off the competition to win bronze in the same event.

42e—Verb Tenses

a.   I will have walked.

b.   I walked.

c.   I had been walking.

d.   I am walking.

e.   I will be walking.

42e–g—Verb Tense, Mood, and Voice

a.   Joan of Arc was a French military leader in the fifteenth century who said that God spoke to her in voices.

b.   Correct.

c.   If Joan of Arc had lived in the twenty-first century, her videos probably would have gone viral.

d.   I wish that time travel were possible, so I could meet her.

e.   It would be interesting to meet Joan of Arc.

43—Singular and Plural Subjects   [Singular   Plural]

a.   Gargoyles were used on many buildings during the Middle Ages.

b.   A gargoyle is a sculpture depicting a grotesque or fantastic creature.

c.   Measles can be deadly.

d.   The jury voted "guilty" and "not guilty" in equal numbers on the first vote.

e.   Anyone who has something to say should speak up now.

43—Subject–Verb Agreement

a.   George Lucas's *Star Wars* has had several sequels.

b.   Some of the buses are overheated.

c.   Correct.

d. The worst part of riding a bus is the waiting.

e. Two dollars is the current bus fare.

44a–i—Pronoun–Antecedent Agreement and Pronoun Reference

a. I expect to find something interesting in any song credited to Lennon and McCartney, but I'm no fan of what Paul McCartney wrote after John Lennon's death.

b. I like to study biological trivia; biology is my major.

c. In Saskatchewan, people say that the cold is a dry cold.

d. Correct.

e. The band put away their instruments.

44j–s—Pronoun Case

a. John, Zara, and I ate the pizza.

b. The anchovies were ordered by Zara and me.

c. We anchovy lovers spare no effort to get our favourite condiment included in the order.

d. Correct.

e. The next pizza may be a joint effort by only Zara and me, however.

45—Adjectives

a. The old computer is unreliable.

b. My father is thrifty and conservative.

c. The desktop—old, outdated, and decrepit—belongs to my father.

d. It was a fast computer when he first bought it.

e. It holds many files he still needs for work.

45—Adverbs

a. The fireplace was very hot.

b. The high temperature for that day was twenty below zero.

c. We regularly pushed huge maple logs into the fireplace.

d. The wind rattled the windowpanes, and the snow swirled fiercely outside the house.

e. The bare trees swayed ominously in the twilight.

45b–e —Using Adjectives and Adverbs

a. Correct.

b. There was no way to hurry the tortoise.

c. This tortoise is really slow.

d.   The tortoise in the Metro Zoo is the ugliest tortoise I've ever seen.

e.   That ugly tortoise also smells bad.

46—Sentence Fragments (Possible answers)

a.   Correct.

b.   Today, *girl* denotes a female child. In Middle English, *girl* denoted a child of either sex. [the present-tense verb *denotes* is also correct]

c.   The word *balkanization* derives from the name of the Balkan Peninsula, which was divided into several small nations in the early twentieth century.

d.   Bacteria, at times present in incorrectly canned or preserved foods, causes botulism, a type of food poisoning which is often fatal if not treated properly.

e.   The title character in *Prince of Persia* was played by Jake Gyllenhaal.

47—Comma Splices and Fused Sentences (Possible answers)

a.   Although William Lyon Mackenzie King successfully held office longer than any other Canadian prime minister, he left an ambiguous legacy.

b.   The huge majority that John Diefenbaker won for the Progressive Conservatives in 1958 has not left him with a victorious reputation, for only five years later his government collapsed.

c.   Correct.

d.   Pierre Trudeau preceded Turner as prime minister, and Brian Mulroney was the leader who retired in favour of Campbell.

e.   During Diefenbaker's last year in office, writer Peter C. Newman criticized him severely in a book called *Renegade in Power;* the same writer released a book in 2005 that deeply offended Mulroney.

48—Problems with Sentence Shifts (Possible answers)

a.   When I hear people argue over PCs versus Macs, they sound to me like people arguing over their religious beliefs.

b.   Correct.

c.   Standing inside the penalty area allows a soccer goalie to handle the ball.

d.   The Montreal Royals sent the first black player to join a major-league baseball team.

e.   The year 2010 was important because several new networks began competing with Canada's big three wireless corporations then.

49—Misplaced Modifiers

a. Barking loudly, the shepherd's dog ran toward the sheep.

b. Anxious to go home, the shepherd signalled her dog to herd the sheep.

c. Correct.

d. The shepherd had just bought her dog from a neighbouring rancher.

e. The dog diligently herded the sheep home.

50—Conciseness (Possible answers)

a. I liked the movie.

b. Our landlord decided to paint our windowsills.

c. Eight of us share the house.

d. John, a good athlete, wants to play professional football.

e. A backbencher introduced the bill in Parliament.

50—Conciseness (Possible answers)

a. The house was large, old, and drafty.

b. Michael Moore, an American filmmaker, sometimes presents Canada as a utopian society in his movies.

c. The bottom line shows profit or loss.

d. People often use the phrase "bottom line" to mean the determining consideration in a decision.

e. Although Canadians laugh at Michael Moore's portrayal of Canada, they feel flattered by it.

51a–b—Coordination (Possible answers)

a. The French Revolution began in 1789; it ended France's thousand-year monarchy.

b. Louis XVI assembled the Estates General to deal with France's huge debt, and then the common people's part of the Estates General proclaimed itself France's true legislature.

c. Louis protested, so a crowd destroyed the Bastille.

d. A constitutional monarchy was established; some people thought the king would be content.

e. Louis and the queen, Marie Antoinette, tried to leave the country, but they were caught, convicted of treason, and executed.

51c–d—Subordination (Possible answers)

a. The French Revolution, which began in 1789, ended France's thousand-year monarchy.

b. After King Louis XVI assembled the Estates General to deal with France's huge debt, the common people's part of the Estates General proclaimed itself France's true legislature.

c. When King Louis protested, a crowd destroyed the Bastille.

d. Because a constitutional monarchy was established, some people thought the king would be content.

e. When King Louis and the queen, Marie Antoinette, tried to leave the country, they were caught, convicted of treason, and executed.

52a–d—Parallelism (Possible answers)

a. Archimedes was an ancient Greek scientist, mathematician, and inventor.

b. According to legend, Archimedes is supposed to have said "Give me the place to stand and a lever long enough, and I will move the earth" and to have shouted "Eureka!" when he stepped into his bath and realized that he could measure the volume of an object by determining the volume of the water it displaces when submerged.

c. Archimedes discovered the principle of buoyancy, he discovered formulas for calculating the areas of various geometric figures, and he invented the Archimedean screw.

d. According to the principle of buoyancy, boats float and balloons rise because they weigh less than the water or air they displace.

e. Correct.

52e–h—Sentence Variety (Possible answers)

a. John Polanyi won the Nobel Price for his research in chemistry. He is a campaigner for socially conscious science.

b. The crucial experiment succeeded.

c. The experiment succeeded brilliantly.

d. After the team tried another approach, the experiment succeeded.

e. The experiment that we had given up on succeeded.

54b—Choosing Exact Words (Possible answers)

a. My nephew's hands and feet need washing.

b. The basketball player is tall.

c. Her perfume has a wonderful scent.

d. I ate a meal of fish and chips.

e. The cheeseburger costs $14.75.

54d–g—Suitable Language, Figurative Language, Clichés, and Tone (Possible answers)

a. Correct.

b. I think I'll fail accounting.

c. Alexander the Great had an interesting idea when he decided to make Babylon his new capital.

d.   The door wouldn't close because the carpenters had hung it incorrectly.

e.   I've heard that the ambassador has been criticizing our prime minister again.

55—Using Inclusive Language (Possible answers)

a.   Ursula Franklin is a scientist.

b.   The Charter gives every citizen freedom of speech.

c.   Correct, assuming that only men were in the room, or only men were applauding.

d.   All police officers should be honest.

e.   Mike cleaned, took care of the children, and cooked. (*Or,* Mike was a stay-at-home dad: he cleaned, took care of the children, and cooked.)

56—Spelling

a.   Correct.

b.   That strategy has affected the team's success rate.

c.   This is the fourth year in five that the team has had a winning season.

d.   We should compliment the coaches on their success.

e.   In the light of this record, though, the coaches probably won't alter much for next year.

56a—Spelling Plurals

a.   Carl prefers his french fries without ketchup.

b.   He was at two beaches yesterday.

c.   Correct.

d.   He wore shoes, so his feet are fine.

e.   Carl is one of my brothers-in-law.

56b–c—Adding Suffixes and Spelling *ie, ei* Words

a.   The teacher said that Sarah was logically inclined.

b.   I believe I will vote against the honourable member's motion.

c.   Did you paint the ceiling?

d.   Correct.

e.   That was the most forgettable movie I've ever seen.

56d—Spelling Homonyms and Frequently Confused Words

a.   The bride and groom walked down the aisle.

b.   I accept the invitation.

c. I'm intrigued by Freud's idea of the subconscious.

d. Correct.

e. Often, a province's capital is not the province's biggest city.

56d—Spelling Homonyms and Frequently Confused Words

a. I'm out of breath after jogging.

b. Cheese and milk are dairy products.

c. Fold the petition and place it carefully in an envelope.

d. Ann led the marching band yesterday.

e. Correct.

57—Commas

a. Myopia, or nearsightedness, is a visual defect.

b. To myopic people, distant objects appear blurred.

c. A myopic person's eyes focus light in front of the retina, but a nonmyopic person's eyes focus light on the retina.

d. Correct.

e. Myopia, therefore, is a visual defect that ordinarily can be corrected.

57—Commas

a. Although Canada's area is 10 000 000 square kilometres, its population is only about 34 000 000 people. [Commas may be used instead of spaces in these numbers.]

b. Canada produces large quantities of wheat and beef.

c. Much of Canada lies in the harsh northern latitudes.

d. Copper, gold, nickel, and zinc are some of the abundant minerals in Canada's reserves.

e. Correct.

57—Commas

a. Correct.

b. The first is to get a new hard drive for my computer.

c. The next is to pay off my data plan, which got completely out of hand in just a few days following December 31, 2010.

d. Doctors who take the Hippocratic oath pledge to do no harm.

e. We drove 1200 kilometres on Friday. [1,200 and 1 200 are also correct.]

58—Semicolons

a. The committee included Ravi Diaram, the new accountant; Sarah Jarna, the coordinator of the advertising division; and Tracy Youngblood, the director of public relations.

b. I enjoy discussing trivia, especially about Canadian celebrities, and reading Canadian, American, and British poetry; nevertheless, I spend most of my spare time earning money to pay for tuition.

c. Susan Musgrave is a well-known poet; however, many people first heard about her when her husband, also a writer, was arrested for bank robbery.

d. Musgrave, who is from British Columbia, says she discovered that she was a "misfit" at an early age; her kindergarten teacher expelled her for laughing in class. [A colon is also correct here.]

e. Correct. [A colon is also correct here.]

59—Colons

a. Correct.

b. Take the 7:05 commuter train to Union Station.

c. Unless there is further political reform, I can already predict the result: another minority government.

d. Governments in Canada are under constant pressure to promote national unity, fund health care adequately, and assert Canada's presence in the United Nations.

e. The original Greek text of John 1:1 has never been adequately translated. [MLA style recommends a period but recognizes the colon as customary.]

58–59—Semicolons and Colons

a. Although David Cronenberg appears on many lists of the world's greatest film directors, early in his career he directed advertisements and short features for television.

b. The advertisements included spots for Ontario Hydro, a running shoe company, and even a brand of chocolate bar.

c. Cronenberg's films have seldom attracted mainstream audiences; nevertheless, *A History of Violence* earned him popular success and an armful of awards.

d. Atom Egoyan has made a long list of acclaimed dramatic films, including *The Sweet Hereafter, The Adjuster, Speaking Parts, Exotica,* and *Ararat.*

e. Correct.

60—Apostrophes

a. Nunavut's area is two million square kilometres.

b. Correct.

c. As the newest territory in Canada's north, Nunavut has attracted the attention of many Canadians.

d. It's easy to imagine all the challenges facing this territory's leaders.

e. The government of Nunavut is responsible to all of its people, but it has a special duty to protect the Inuit people's lands and culture.

61—Quotation Marks

a. I am reading a short story by Robertson Davies, "The Charlottetown Banquet."

b. An item on Feist's website reads: "We are beyond pleased to report that on April 29, a flash mob of 300 dancers infiltrated the public concourse of the Eaton Centre, Toronto, with a mass dance to Feist's 'Feel It All' remix by Escort."

c. Many people confuse "lie" and "lay." [Use of italics (underlining) is also correct for words used as words, and is recommended MLA style.]

d. The music programmer told me, "This group's 'new' sound comes from sampling old material from its own bestselling album."

e. Correct.

62— Periods, Question Marks, and Exclamation Marks

a. In 1968 Pierre Trudeau proclaimed his intention to make Canada a "just society."

b. Correct.

c. I asked my professor if this was true.

d. She confirmed my idea, but unfortunately, she suggested that I analyze the differences between the two slogans in my mid-term paper.

e. How do you think I should approach that? From the point of view of individual personality? national traditions? social problems? linguistic and racial issues?

63—Other Punctuation Marks

a. Correct.

b. Some bacteria—those that live in the digestive tract and aid digestion, for example—are beneficial to humans.

c. Regrettably, we cannot endorse an annual report containing erroneous statements such as "Our profits for this fiscal year amounted to $20 trillion [sic], a figure we were hoping to improve on."

d. In her poem "Chahinkapa Zoo," Louise Erdrich writes about the frustration wild animals in zoos must feel (but can animals really feel frustration?); the poem begins, "It is spring. Even here / The bears emerge from poured caverns. / Already their cubs have been devoured / by the feather-footed lynx caged next door."

e. Erdrich's zoo is a nasty place in which the bears' "cubs have been devoured / by the . . . lynx caged next door."

64—Hyphens

a. Correct.

b. "Self-love" is one way to translate the French expression *amour propre*.

c. Each of the graduated bowls that make a glass harmonica will produce a bell-like tone of a particular pitch when you press your finger to its moistened rim.

d. The play director asked all cast members to re-dress for a group picture.

e. The more expensive coat is the better looking coat.

65—Capitals

a. Ursula Franklin has been a research scientist, a university professor, and an antiwar activist.

b. Correct.

c. After leaving her research position, Franklin (1) became the first female professor in her university department, (2) worked on the application of physics and chemistry to archaeology, and (3) joined the Royal Society of Canada.

d. In 2002, the United Nations Association in Canada awarded her the Pearson Peace Medal.

e. Franklin has said that "in the post–September 11 world, it is doubly important to explore the means of peace and cooperation because in the face of violence, one forgets so easily the solutions . . . that were achieved without war."

66—Italics (Underlining)

a. Correct. [MLA style prefers underlining to represent italic text.]

b. We flew in a Dash 8 commuter jet named *The City of Ottawa*.

c. The decreases in our foreign-aid budget have left many Canadians deeply disappointed.

d. Canada's oldest weekly news magazine is *Maclean's*.

e. Leonard Cohen's "Suzanne" is both a poem and a song.

67—Abbreviations

a. While discussing the pessimism so pervasive in the fourteenth century (AD 1300–1399), Barbara Tuchman writes in her book *A Distant Mirror*, "Death is not treated poetically as the soul's flight to reunion with God; it is a skeleton grinning at the vanity of life." [Periods are also correct: A.D. 1300–1399.]

b. Correct.

c.   Dr. Bette Stephenson gave up her medical practice to run for the provincial legislature.

d.   Canada participated in the Boer War, the First World War, and others, but not in the 2003 invasion of Iraq.

e.   The application was sent to 2200 Wascana Road, in Saskatoon.

68—Numbers

a.   Bart Simpson and his family first appeared on TV on April 19, 1987.

b.   Correct.

c.   Uranium's melting point is 1132°C, and its boiling point is 3818°C. [1,132°C and 3,818°C, and 1 132°C and 3 818°C are also correct.]

d.   During my shift, I received thirty-five 911 calls.

e.   The department office opens at nine o'clock every weekday morning.

69a—Count and Noncount Nouns   [Count   Noncount]

a.   Hot <u>air</u> rises.

b.   Hot air <u>balloons</u> rise.

c.   I packed my <u>clothing</u> in the <u>suitcase</u>.

d.   I packed my <u>equipment</u> in the <u>bag</u>.

e.   Do you speak <u>French</u>?

69a, 42a–c, 43a—Singulars and Plurals

a.   My birthday is two days away.

b.   Ice is cold.

c.   Correct.

d.   My shoes are wet.

e.   Gasoline is expensive in Nunavut.

69b—Singulars and Plurals

a.   Does she live in the big house on the corner?

b.   I live in an apartment near here.

c.   Tomatoes are tasty in salads.

d.   Correct.

e.   He has a few sheets of paper.

70—Articles

a. It was an honour to receive an award.

b. The beaver, our national animal, is easy to find in Canada, although the lion, which is the United Kingdom's national animal, is rarely seen there.

c. My dream is to have a chalet on Lake Louise.

d. Cats are animals that many people keep as pets.

e. Correct.

71—Word Order

a. Will Sasha take Anastasia to the concert?

b. Are my new blue slacks in the closet?

c. Yesterday, I bought the last three tickets for the concert.

d. We've never heard this band before.

e. Correct.

71b–c, 45—Adjectives and Adverbs   [Adjective   Adverb]

a. I quickly ate the two eggs.

b. I drank orange juice first, and then I ate two eggs.

c. He devoured the fresh eggs rapidly.

d. The yolks of these free-range eggs are bright yellow.

e. We never eat raw eggs.

72—Prepositions

a. Correct.

b. We'll meet Mario and Sidney at the hockey game.

c. Before we go in, we'll check for our tickets.

d. We need to get off the bus.

e. Look out for vehicles when we run across the street.

73—Gerunds and Infinitives   [Gerund   Infinitive]

a. We like to play cards after lunch.

b. We particularly enjoy playing bridge.

c. Do you promise to play bridge sometime?

d. We plan to play cards again on Friday.

e. We will try to play for an hour.

73—Gerunds and Infinitives

a. Nicole cannot help hating mosquitoes.

b. As for me, I refuse to be bothered by them.

c. Why should I be unable to tolerate such tiny insects?

d. Nicole, however, won't risk going outside on lovely summer evenings.

e. She just can't seem to agree to put on full-body mosquito netting as I do.

74—Modal Auxiliary Verbs

a. I can work in the kitchen.

b. I cannot work in the kitchen.

c. I (should, ought to) work in the kitchen.

d. I would rather work in the kitchen.

e. I (used to, would) work in the kitchen.

Review 1 (Possible answers)

a. A bartender makes cocktails.

b. Correct.

c. Even though her name is Emma, she prefers to use the name Amina.

d. The lion is an animal well designed for stalking, for chasing, and for overpowering its prey.

e. The elephant trumpeted in triumph when it defeated its opponent.

Review 2

a. After the mixture boils for five minutes, it cools in the test tube.

b. If people in the country went shopping for a new car tomorrow, would they generally buy or lease?

c. The batter struck out, and in the blink of an eye the catcher threw the ball to first base.

d. I got lost because I was unfamiliar with the neighbourhood.

e. Correct.

Review 3: Multilingual Writers

a. Jann has just scheduled her next two major concert appearances.

b. I have not listened to her new album yet.

c. Correct.

d. I am thinking of taking piano lessons soon.

e. I can afford them because I have a little money saved to hire a piano teacher.

Review 4

a. Several famous boxers have taken the nickname "Sugar Ray."

b. "Brillig" is a nonsense word that was coined by Lewis Carroll.

c. Correct.

d. The exam is scheduled for 2:45.

e. The National Gallery, which operates under the 1990 Museums Act, is required to develop, maintain, and make known Canadian art.

Review 5

a. Compare the search results with Google and Yahoo.

b. The bear walked back and forth all day long in its cage.

c. A well-balanced diet includes foods from all the major food groups.

d. When Little Red Riding Hood comments on her grandmother's big teeth, the wolf (who is disguised as the grandmother) replies, "The better to eat you with!"

e. Correct.